FROM THE
GROUND UP

FROM THE GROUND UP

NEW TESTAMENT FOUNDATIONS
FOR THE 21ST-CENTURY CHURCH

J. SCOTT HORRELL

Kregel
Academic & Professional

From the Ground Up: New Testament Foundations for the 21st-Century Church

Published by Kregel Publications, a division of Kregel, Inc., P.O. Box 2607, Grand Rapids, MI 49501. Kregel Publications provides trusted, biblical publications for Christian growth and service.

Library of Congress Cataloging-in-Publication Data
Horrell, John Scott.
    From the ground up: New Testament foundations for the 21st century church /by J. Scott Horrell.
        p.   cm.
    1. Church—Biblical teaching. 2. Church—21st century.
I. Title.
BS2545.C5H67 2004
262—dc22   2004019249

ISBN 0-8254-2891-2

Printed in the United States of America

1 2 3 4 5 / 08 07 06 05 04

CONTENTS

Preface 7
Introduction: Running in Circles, Running Down 11

1. Appearance and Substance: *Church* in Scripture 19
2. What Is the Universal Church? 29
3. Centered in Christ, Decentralized in the World 41
4. What Happened? An Abbreviated Tour Through
   Church History 53
5. What Is the Local Church? 63
6. What We Do Reveals Who We Are: Functioning as Church 73
7. Road Posts Toward a New Testament Church 87

Conclusion: The End or a New Beginning? 99
Appendix: Four Functions or More? 101
Suggested Reading 105
Scripture Index 107

111137

PREFACE

Recently I sat in a stone church building that occupies a full city block on some of the most expensive real estate in my adopted city of Dallas, Texas. Like several other churches embellishing the neighborhood, this church employs a large staff to care for the ornate decor, manicure the grounds, and coordinate the many church-related activities. While a few congregations may flourish, other notable churches face financial crises, the church leaders calling on members to rescue their buildings yet again from dilapidation if not bankruptcy. Ironically, in their efforts to build and maintain their *facilities*, few members of these churches— growing or struggling—pause to wonder whether their understanding of what the *church* is supposed to be may be misguided.

The concept that a church building and pastoral staff are the center of God's work in the world is endemic not only to large traditional institutions but also to nearly every congregation in the world. The building may be humble and outdated in appearance or it may be gigantic and shiny new, like a neo-Pentecostal center in Brazil that boasts room for more than 100,000 worshipers. But whether the architecture is contemporary or historic (steeple and all), the theology behind it is much the same—it often reflects a Byzantine or European orientation to the church edifice as the temple of God.

The disparity between traditional ways of being the church (however old or new that tradition might be) and the church as portrayed in the

New Testament is striking. In most Western churches today, the members' gifts and resources are channeled primarily toward building and staffing institutional centers. The purpose is to establish a base of worship, with occasional forays to help the poor and to reach those who are without Christ. Moreover, God has used this kind of church, as history demonstrates, within the wide plurality of his people.

Nevertheless, as one involved in planting churches in other countries, I confess a great unease with what we have conceived as "the church," and how we in the West—or, more specifically, in the North Atlantic countries—have passed these ideas on to people of other cultures. Cathedrals have multiplied around the world, constructed first with European blueprints—not only in terms of architecture but also in the very concepts of church—and then these ideas are copied by nationals as authentic Christian faith. One might think that the decline of European and American Christendom would be a cautionary tale. In far too many cities, elaborate church buildings stand as lifeless monuments to the Christian faith, representing millions of dollars and tens of thousands of hours of invested lives.

How did our Lord design the church? The Bible speaks of a spiritual unity of all who have been regenerated, or born of the Spirit. It calls this reality "the body of Christ." The particular expressions of the universal church are found especially in local churches, with all their humanness, fragility, and cultural conditions. The implications of such simple New Testament teachings are remarkably liberating.

As we enter the third millennium, many Christians sense an increasing dissonance between the ways we have "done church" and the changing cultural environment, wherever we might live in the modern world. Part of this discord owes to a moral devolution across many of the world's cultures. Regardless of how we understand the "last days" described in the New Testament, there are not many reasons to think the world will be Christianized when Christ returns. So one reason local churches will never "fit" well in the world is because vital biblical faith, in one sense, exists as an aroma of death to those who do not know the Savior. The gospel of Jesus Christ contradicts the values of the nonbelieving world. However, another reason for the disconnection between the church and the unbelieving people to whom it is called may be our own misunderstandings of what the church is or should be. This is as true in Manila and Cairo as it is in Chicago.

How should we think of the church? Not everything in Scripture is transparent about how Christians should live out this miracle of "the body of Christ." But certainly the pattern is clear. In this book we shall attempt to readjust our concept of what the church is called to be according to the New Testament. Much will not be new, nor should it be. Yet old vines need paring away and new vines need fastening to the framework of God's Word.

I should warn you that reactions to the message of this book have been strong, both inside and outside North America. Seminarians and those working to establish new churches have applauded its message, whereas denominational leaders sometimes have not. Our preconceptions run deep and are forged by our experiences; this is as true for me as it is the next person. And, not uncommonly, we profess one ecclesiology but live quite another. Our Lord has shown immeasurable mercy through two thousand years of Christian faith, even as the church has wandered through forms and appearances quite distant from New Testament parameters. May this small volume help inspire a return to the fold—that is, to conceiving and to *living out* the doctrine of the church in harmony with the life of the Spirit of Christ *within*.

RUNNING IN CIRCLES, RUNNING DOWN

Processionary caterpillars feed on flowers and leaves as they move in long lines across the jungle floor. Each butts its head against the extremity of the one before it. And so life goes on.

Studying a group of processionary caterpillars, the French naturalist Jean-Henri Fabre induced them onto the mouth of a large vase. Uniting the last caterpillar with the first, Fabre formed a living circle with neither beginning nor end. He supposed that after a while the caterpillars would tire of their repetitious march, break their useless cycle, and set off in a new direction. This, however, was not the case. The caterpillars continued at the same velocity on the same futile path, hour after hour, night and day.[1]

After several days, a favorite food was deliberately placed near the vase where it could be sensed by the caterpillars but not within immediate reach of the circle. Even then, each habitually followed the one before it. The caterpillars refused to vary from their routine, persisting instead on the same trajectory—day after day—in what became for them a march of death.

---

1. Jean-Henri Casimir Fabre, *The Life of the Caterpillar*, trans. Alexander Louis Teixeira de Mattos (Toronto: McClelland, Goodchild and Stewart, 1916).

The processionary caterpillars were following past experience, instinct, tradition, precedent, custom, established pattern, what they had always done. But they were following blindly. They confused *activity* with *progress*. Despite their best intentions, persistence, and fortitude, these processionary caterpillars were going to die.

So it is, too often, with the church. Many times we recall with gratitude our past experiences in the presence of the Lord. With nostalgia, we remember the zeal of our youth group, powerful evangelistic services, or certain choruses and hymns of the faith that have touched us deeply. Most of us were brought up in and molded by church traditions that we appreciate, sometimes deeply. We yearn for others in the church to experience *today* the same consecration and aliveness in Christ that we have known. Nevertheless, when we try to repeat in the present what was done in the past, our activities lack the same power. Earlier forms of Christian vitality do not always reach new generations. The tried-and-true evangelistic methods of old evoke from our neighbors today little more than a disinterested yawn—or, even worse, revulsion, given the current cultural stereotypes regarding Christian believers. Forms of worship and evangelism that once meant so much to us now seem meaningless as we seek to communicate to a different generation and to people of differing social backgrounds. Despite concerted efforts by our leaders, our church programs too often become mere habit with the passing of years, without the force to penetrate the lives of the people sitting in the pews. Nor is this declension limited to traditional denominations. It characterizes more than a few independent and pentecostal churches as well. We continue with our forms and methods because they have worked in the past, with the expectation that they will continue to work in the future. More than we imagine, we have become processionary caterpillars.

Old Ways and Very Old Ways

One cannot help but notice a significant tension between the traditional way of being the church and what we encounter in the Bible. Many of the forms and practices in today's local churches simply do not fit with what the church in the New Testament did and set out to do. The suspicion is that the customs, patterns, and organization of our churches today sometimes act as barriers to the very purpose of the church. The usual way of being the church might, in fact, defeat what the church is all about as designed by God. And the tension cannot simply be attributed to traditional versus contemporary, conservative versus progressive, or High Church versus Gen-X church styles. The issues are far more foundational. As Christians, we say that the Bible—especially the New Testament—is the basis of our faith and practice as local churches. Yet our ecclesiological heritage—how we do church with all our traditions and structures—reveals a mixture of practices, some of which stand considerably outside the realm of the New Testament.

Four Common Church Conceptions

Over the past decade, a group of pastors in São Paulo, Brazil, has concluded that the majority of activities in their own churches—which are typical of tens of thousands of churches around the world—revolve around four central images:

1. The church building or "temple"
2. Sunday, the "Christian Sabbath"
3. The worship service
4. The full-time pastor[2]

When people think of the local church, their understanding orients around these four controlling concepts. Let's look more closely at each one.

A Church Building

First, to be a church means to have real estate—land and a building—and the bigger the better. Be it a storefront in a strip mall or a forty-acre,

---

2. Ed René Kivitz, *Quebrando Paradigmas* (São Paulo: Abba, 1995), 37–56; and various ongoing pastors' discussions in São Paulo to the present. See also *Ultrapassando Barreiras*, ed. J. Scott Horrell, 2 vols. (São Paulo: Vida Nova, 1994–95).

multimillion-dollar campus, the church building is viewed as "the house of God," the Christian "temple," a kind of residence or activity center for the Christian family. An edifice gives visibility and permanence. If it is new, we feel good about it. If it's old, we are a bit embarrassed (unless it is very old, and then we feel proud again). Without a building, a group of Christians is hardly noticed; it's like a migrant passing through town, unheeded or disregarded by folks who live there. Consciously or not, in most people's thinking, the church building is central. What we *give* to God, we give there. What we *do* for God, we especially do there. To serve God is to serve in the church. For many Christians, that means as much *where* we serve as *what* we might accomplish.

Sunday

Second, to be a church is to "keep the Sabbath," the day on which we worship and do service to the Lord. A Sunday Sabbath is a reality expressed more explicitly in other parts of the world than in North America today. In Jerusalem, London, and Nairobi, for example, Muslims worship on Friday, Jews on Saturday, and Christians on Sunday. Yet, the priority of Sunday worship, while not the Sabbatarian legalism of the past, remains a binding tradition in North American churches as well. When a person does something for God on a day other than Sunday ("the Lord's Day"), he or she rather feels it is something extra—a kind of tip for God. Of course, most people would never say such a thing. But subconsciously, beyond Sunday and an occasional church event at Christmas or Easter, many feel as if they have put in religious overtime. Now God might even owe them something.

Worship Service

Third, to be a church means to have a worship service—the spiritual apex of the week. The worship service is where a person meets God and where God reaches the lost. For many, the weekly worship gathering is the life generator of the congregation. It empowers members for the weekly battle. It is the measure of a church's strength and effectiveness.

At the worship service, the spirituality of the church is at stake. Preparation occurs all week long (or weeks in advance), so that the music, drama, testimonies, and preaching will be as smooth and convincing as possible. Though we do not often say it, we rather assume that the worship service is God's platform and performance, the one big weekly opportunity to penetrate people's lives.

A church building, a Sunday-centered Christian life, and a high-octane worship service—these characteristics define what hundreds of millions of believers conceive to be a church, and a *good* church. As they reflected on their own congregations, the Brazilian leaders included all these and one other important mark of what most people expect of a *real* church.

Full-time Pastor

In much of the world, to be a church means to have a full-time pastor. In traditional parlance, the pastor is "the man of God"—the leader, prophet, mediator, comforter, and shepherd of his sheep. The *pastor* and, better still, *pastors* (*important* churches have more than one) are the ones who take us to God and who bring God to us. Different from the rest of us, pastors have been trained for ministry. They understand God better than we do. Pastors know how to do church right. Without a professional pastor, a church is not a complete church.

While admitting exaggerations in the above statements, the São Paulo leaders (themselves pastors) concluded that this is how vast numbers of Evangelicals in Latin America understand the church. Others attest that this is also very much the case in Africa, Asia, and Europe. I suspect the same ideas represent preconceptions in most North American congregations as well. While we give lip service to other definitions of the church, our practice is quite different. If any one or two of these elements are missing—a building, Sunday observance, a central worship service, or a professional pastor—then most of us wonder whether we truly have a church at all. Or in any case, we suppose that our church is not what it *should* be. In actuality, as we will see, our thinking about the church often reflects, surprisingly, more of the Old Testament than the New Testament.

Why Read This Book

What you hold in your hand serves as a biblical primer, a kind of theological *brief* on the essence of the church. The work is born out of missionary efforts to build Christ's church in cultures quite distant from the more established churches of North America. In that sense, this little book is meant to serve as a church-planting guidebook in situations that call for innovative, yet firmly biblical, thinking. In another sense, these chapters are addressed to all who lack time (or interest) to wade through detailed tomes on ecclesiology but to whom the subject remains significant—indeed vital—to life. You may be involved in church leadership as a businessman inundated with other involvements, yet you sometimes wonder what the church is all about. You've wondered how you can strengthen the local church when in your mind the whole point of church isn't particularly clear. You may be a pastor desiring to pull back from a heavy schedule to reconsider an ecclesial administration that has become unwieldy and (if the truth be known) depressing. Or you may be in a Bible study and wondering what the church should be, or even struggling with what kind of a church to attend. This short book will not resolve the particulars of how a church should look, nor will it discuss theologies of baptism, the Lord's Supper, the attributes of a leader, or church discipline. It serves as only a thumbnail sketch of the biblical contours of what Christ's church is designed to be—and thus, in an inverted sense, also what the local church should *not* be.

Our study defines the essence of the church in light of the New Testament and aids the reader in evaluating current church practices in that light. Our priority is the definition of *church*, particularly as it pertains to the universal church and the local congregation. The *universal church*, or body of Christ, is part of the unity and diversity of a greater number of God's people; thus, the unique characteristics of the church, as well as its continuity with all of salvation history, are crucial for our thinking. Ideally, the *local church* will be a tangible expression of the body of Christ, with its primary activities well established in the New Testament. We will conclude with suggestions for how to better conceive and align our local churches with the primary emphases of the early church, while thinking creatively about our twenty-first-century contexts. If we say that our local churches are built on the Word of God, it may be an occasion to reevaluate the many artifacts that have piled high in the church basement and now fill the parking lot. We may discover that the New Testament sets us free in the local church to more effectively be the body of Christ in the midst of a needy yet indifferent world.

Please understand that I am not a malcontent who has thrown off tradition and normalcy for the fringes of Christian faith. I speak from the belly of the whale, having pastored five times and taught in theological seminaries in several cultures of the world. Whether in pastors' conferences or seminary lectures, I find that students and pastors alike yearn for a way out of what has become a black hole of administration and activities that, rather than replenishing life in Christ and the fullness of the Spirit, has sucked our churches dry, leadership and all. Too often our churches are but shells of what the Lord of the church has intended. God has designed the church to build up not only new believers but veterans and church leaders as well.

In the New Testament, the church is called the body of Christ. Such a concept carries extraordinary implications for how we should understand the local church today. Our need is to re-experience the ecclesiological freedom and creative vigor of the New Testament. A biblical ecclesiology allows us to experiment with new forms of the local church that appear very different from the historical and denominational patterns with which most of us are familiar. This is not to say that the forms of existing churches are necessarily wrong. God has given us considerable latitude regarding the form and organization of the local church. But one thing is clear: many local churches today appear quite different from what we see in the early church. Modernity and cultural distinctions will inevitably separate us from the early church—and that is right and good. But too often the indispensable elements of New Testament church life are lacking in our contemporary institutions. Having not answered clearly the questions of *why* the church exists and *what* it is supposed to do, we continue in our habits like the church next door and the one down the street. We continue as processionary caterpillars.

Chapter 1

APPEARANCE AND SUBSTANCE

CHURCH IN SCRIPTURE

The Important and the Unimportant

Getting Perspective. There are two paradoxical truths.

On the one hand, the forms and structures of the local church are not particularly important. Our ecclesiastical organization, architecture, music, dress, and order of service are mere means to an end. The power of the gospel of Jesus Christ and the workings of the Holy Spirit are far more central and important than the external forms of our churches, the pottery through which the triune God operates. In a primary sense, it does not matter which organization or denominational label a local church employs. Where there is preaching of biblical truth, where there is faith and commitment, where people seek God's presence and expect answers in prayer, where people obey the Word and overcome sin, there the living God is at work in mercy and power. The most old-fashioned fundamentalist church may be alive with the presence of the Lord Jesus. The noisy, spontaneous, "Holy Ghost" worship service of Pentecostalism may be equally alive, where there is fidelity to our Savior. And the silent worship and recitation of the Apostles' Creed in High Church liturgy may also be saturated with wonderful adoration to the Most High God. As reformers Martin Luther and John Calvin insisted, the true church is centered on the Word and the Spirit. The church is where Jesus Christ is glorified, the Spirit is active, and believers' hearts are kindled with love and zeal. This is what we yearn for. To the contrary, throughout Christian history when the church has become preoccupied with itself—its own appearance and organization—it has suffered spiritual anemia. Forms, methodologies, and rituals occupy a secondary place in the New Testament. External to the spiritual life of the church, structure and appearance are simply not that important.

On the other hand, paradoxically, the study of the church with its forms and organization is enormously important. Certain practices prescribed by the New Testament are essential for all local churches. At the very least, they must include qualified leadership, water baptism, and the Lord's Supper. Biblical steps for church discipline are also well established. Such forms are nonnegotiable for any church at any time. Moreover, it hardly needs to be said that every local church must possess *some* kind of structure. The local church, therefore, may be likened to the body and soul of the human being.

As Athanasius, the fourth-century church father, said in quite a different context, the *finite* cannot contain the *infinite*. He was speaking of the Incarnation of our Savior. Our Lord's humanity could not contain all that is the eternal Son of God, yet it is through this single human figure, Jesus Christ, that God's radiant splendor is expressed with overwhelming power.[1] How ironic that scholars know almost nothing about what Jesus actually looked like. His physical form, by which salvation was brought to the world, is not described in the earliest Christian records. Likewise, the local church must have its own flesh and blood, forms and appearance, to live as the body of Christ in the world. This is the mystery of the Incarnation, the deep truth of the hypostatic union of our Lord's two natures in one united person. Our humanity is such that we need a finite, corporeal form to do anything at all. Without bodies, how could we express ourselves? How would our inner reality be known? And yet we are far more than our bodies.

So it is with the local church. Without patterns and plans, how could any group of people function? Forms are *essential* to a congregation's existence in order to organize and facilitate the Lord's purposes in the

---

1. St. Athanasius, *On the Incarnation,* trans. and ed. C. S. M. V., with an introduction by C. S. Lewis (Crestwood, N.Y.: St. Vladimir's Seminary Press, 1998), 45–47 (3.17–18).

lives of its members. Through social structures, we relate to one another and to the non-Christian society around us. Consequently, though God's truth and power are far greater than the finite structures of the local church in which they operate, those little structures are still God's loudspeakers to the world. In one sense, then, the form of the local church isn't particularly important. In another, only our church's form—our visible way of being—enables us to express our inner spiritual life. Earthen vessels are God's means of accomplishing his will in this world.

Appearance and Message

In light of the Incarnation, the visible image of the local church announces to the world the kind of God we say we worship. Consider your own local assembly. How would a stranger perceive God based on the appearance and style of your congregational meetings? Set aside doctrinal statements for the moment and imagine yourself as a stranger entering your church's Sunday service. What is the atmosphere, the feeling, of your main gathering? Is God mellow and rather conservative? Is he a spiritual dictator over passive sheep? Is he always smiling and seeking to be accepted by people? Does God, as expressed through your congregation, appear austere and distant, the type of God that doesn't especially like people? Is he a celestial master of ceremonies, presiding over shouts and dances and hallelujahs? Is he a fashionable suburban God who assuredly desires your financial welfare? Is he perhaps a self-effacing, postmodern God, quietly hoping someone will believe? Or is he predictable and, frankly, rather boring? Remember, this is the God whose presence we invoke at the outset of the service, the one to whom our prayers and music are addressed, the one whose Word we expound, whose will we exhort, and whose blessing we publicly seek.

What impressions does our church give of its Lord to the casual onlooker? Does our God seem disorganized? or is he ultra-organized? Is God ethnic, or does he accept all peoples? Does God only want our money, or does he care for the homeless and poor? Does he like the formal and traditional, or does he prefer the contemporary and upbeat? Is he tolerant or intolerant? Is God impressed by suits and fashionable dress, or is he laid-back, content with blue jeans and T-shirts? Is God largely intellectual, or does he run on emotions? Is he judgmental, with lists of rules? or is he easy on sin, with nothing particularly bothering him? Is God patriotic, preferring a national flag on each side of the cross? Through the forms, patterns, and styles of our local church, we broadcast volumes about the nature of the God we claim to serve. Unfortunately, it is too often these external realities that most obscure the good news of Jesus Christ.

The observable form of a local church represents its God to the world. So, although it is not the most important aspect of what the church is all about, our conclusions about the form of the church are extremely important. The appearance of the local church proclaims to observers—Buddhists, Muslims, agnostics, and the utterly undefined—much more about our concept of God than we might expect. With shouting, miracle-working preachers on one television channel, and formal, liturgical services on another, is it any wonder that the Christian population of India has dropped from four percent in 1980 to just over two percent in a government census at the turn of the century? Or that an intelligent woman in Paris or Munich might have a simply awful concept of Christian faith because of the forms of Christianity she has known? Although the church does not exist for the benefit of unbelievers, in an increasingly cosmopolitan world, the local church may say more by its outward forms than we would ever want to express.

And let us not forget that outward appearance also influences those who are *inside* the church. From architecture to music, from dress to ritual (whether formal or not), from our "business meetings" to collecting the offering, our church forms are replete with implications that touch the life of every believer. A megawatt performance in an auditorium may produce a momentary adrenaline kick that is never quite equaled in the silence of personal devotion. A pastor's Cadillac or Mercedes lifestyle will surely set the standard of aspiration for his congregation. Traditional hymns and worn-out choruses in a conservative church, however spiritual its members, may instill in its youth a sense of hopelessness at ever reaching their postmodern friends. Arching spires, choirs, and classical art may stimulate aesthetic awe and praise in a university student, but after graduation she may find it hard to worship God in a drab brick church in rural Nebraska.

Consciously or not, the appearance and form of our local churches shape the way we think as Christians—our aesthetic, our preferences, our patterns of life. The reality is inescapable. We teach far more than the lesson on Sunday morning. Too often our local churches inculcate (unwittingly) subcultures that become part of the problem rather than a means for achieving the Lord's purpose. With time, our experiences harden into presuppositions about how God supposedly works in our lives and others.

In truth, we cannot entirely escape our culturally defined boundaries. Nevertheless, we can wend our way through the cultural–traditional thicket toward becoming a Christlike local church by utilizing two processes of self-evaluation. The first involves simply stepping back and reflecting on what our local church communicates about God through its way of being. We might identify those aspects of our church that genuinely reveal the triune God to our congregation and the surrounding community. Then we should isolate any components of our local church's form and appearance that may actually thwart what we desire to communicate about our Lord. Our study will return to deepen these investigations.

The second process calls us back to Scripture. Ironically, we may find that the New Testament prescribes *less* than we usually assume regarding what the local church must look like. Battles in church history over proper organization, rituals, or visible expressions of faith more often revolve around early *patterns* of church governance and ritual than on mandates in God's Word. Nevertheless, the New Testament does communicate quite a lot about what the local church should *do*.

We turn now to evaluate in some depth the meanings of *church* in the Bible. Through a better definition of the church, we can move toward *being* a church that better reflects our God and Savior.

Down to Bedrock: The Church in Scripture

In a cover story evaluating Christianity in Europe, a recent international issue of *Time* magazine asked the question, "Where Did God Go?"[2] The authors observed that the stone and stained-glass edifices of the Chartres and Notre Dame cathedrals attract far more tourists than worshipers in

---

2. Jeff Chu, "O Father Where Art Thou?" *Time,* 16 June 2003, 18–26.

the twenty-first century. A map charting European Christianity was titled "In the Church but Not in the Church." The article noted that 83 percent of the population of Great Britain belongs to a religious denomination but only 18.4 percent attend services at least once a month. In France, 57.5 percent belong to a denomination, but only twelve percent attend services; in Russia, 50.5 percent belong but only 9.1 percent attend; and in Italy, whereas 82.2 percent are church members, 53.7 percent claim to attend church at least monthly. But what does the term *church* mean? As in the article, most people assume a kind of double meaning of *church:* both a denominational affiliation and a church building where believers engage in corporate worship.

When we speak of *Christian* churches, however, we would be wise to ask what does the New Testament say about church? What is its divine design in terms of purpose and expression? What kind of latitude might local churches have regarding their structure, style, and physical appearance? Our first step is to reexamine the definition of the church in Scripture. We will bore deeply for a few moments, because it is crucial to establish a firm foundation.

If the Christian church has its origins in the Bible, we might rightly suppose that Scripture itself would best define what God intends for our congregations. The English word *church* phonetically derives from the Greek term *kuriakos,* meaning "belonging to the Lord." We use the English *church* to translate the Greek *ekklesia,* literally "those called out" (from *ek kaleo*), although we should not press the word's origins too far. In its classical Greek usage and in the Septuagint (the Greek translation of the Old Testament), *ekklesia* signifies "meeting," "general assembly," "congregation," a group of soldiers, exiles, religious people, or even angels.[3] When we come to the New Testament, for example in Acts 7:38, the word denotes the congregation of Israelites with Moses in the desert (Num. 14:3–4). In Acts 19:32 and 41, *ekklesia* refers to a mob gathered

3. See J. Roloff, "ἐκκλησία," in *Exegetical Dictionary of the New Testament,* ed. H. Balz and G. Schneider, 3 vols. (Grand Rapids: Eerdmans, 1990), 1:410–15; and K. L. Schmidt, "ἐκκλησία," in *Theological Dictionary of the New Testament,* ed. G. Kittel and G. Friedrich, trans. G. W. Bromiley et al., 10 vols. (Grand Rapids: Eerdmans, 1965–76), 3:501–36.

against the apostle Paul in Ephesus. Interestingly, in the same passage (Acts 19:39), the term also refers to the official, juridical assembly that governed Roman cities. A Christian congregation, too, might function like an unruly crowd or a juridical assembly once in a while, but that was not Luke's point as he used the term in these texts in Acts.

Of the 114 occurrences of the word *ekklesia* in the New Testament, almost all of the remaining 110 clearly refer to the Christian church. Except for two verses (Matt. 16:18; 18:17), the term *ekklesia* does not occur in the Gospels.[4] It is not until after Pentecost that we see the conceptual development of the term *church*. The word *ekklesia* is used twenty-three times in the book of Acts; sixty-two times in Paul's letters; twice in Hebrews; once in James; three times in 3 John; and twenty times in Revelation (nineteen times in chapters 1–3). The word is particularly found in Paul (with Luke) and in the words of the resurrected Christ in the book of Revelation. The frequency and use of *ekklesia* in the New Testament is critical to a better understanding of the meaning of the term for our day and for the good of our congregations.

Four Primary Meanings

Of the 110 occurrences of *ekklesia* related to the Christian church, New Testament use divides into four more precise definitions: a gathering, a local church, Christians in a geographical area, and the body of Christ.

Gathering

In some cases, *ekklesia* describes a meeting, reunion, or congregation of Christians (in a sense most like the Old Testament Hebrew word *qahal*): "When you come together in church" (1 Cor. 11:18; cf. 14:4, 19, 28, 34).

---

4. Almost certainly the texts in Matthew are being applied to what became the Christian church. Most scholars agree that the common language of the Jews in Jesus' day was Aramaic. Led by the Spirit, Matthew is probably recording and translating the teaching of Jesus from Aramaic into the language of the New Testament (Koine Greek). Of course he wrote his Gospel well after Pentecost with the New Testament church firmly established. Hebrews 2:12 is a quote from Psalm 22:22 applied to the church.

The idea in these passages does not refer to a place or building but to a convened *assembly* or *gathering* for the purposes of worship and fellowship. Used in this sense, then, when the meeting ends, the *ekklesia* no longer exists. The Bible never uses the word *church* for a building, sanctuary, or temple—unlike today when it is perhaps the term's most frequent connotation in popular language. When we shout, "I'll run over to the church to pick up a bulletin," we use the term in a way the Bible does not. Rather, this first definition of *ekklesia* denotes "the church gathered."

Local Church

The most common biblical use of *ekklesia* describes a congregation or local community of Christians (Acts 8:1; 11:22, 26; Rom. 16:1; James 5:14). In contrast to *ekklesia* as a gathering, here the focus is on the *people* and not so much the meeting. A few times, the apostle Paul mentions the local congregations as plural (1 Cor. 11:16, 22; 1 Tim. 2:14). The majority of the New Testament epistles are addressed to specific local churches (2 Cor. 1:1; 1 Thess. 1:1), as are the messages to the seven churches of Revelation 2–3. Usually, therefore, *ekklesia* defines a local congregation of believers.

Christians in a Geographical Area

Occasionally, *ekklesia* involves the totality of Christians in a geographic region; for example, "the churches in the province of Asia" (1 Cor. 16:19), "the churches in Galatia" (Gal. 1:2), or the singular "the *church* throughout Judea, Galilee and Samaria enjoyed a time of peace" (Acts 9:31). This latter use probably includes all the local churches of a given region, but it also approximates the fourth definition of the universal church discussed below. The concept of church as a *denomination*—the Eastern Orthodox Church, Wesleyan Methodist Church, Reformed Baptist Church—does not exist in the New Testament. When this collective definition of church is found in Scripture, it describes believers in geographic proximity, not doctrinal or organizational distinctions. This is not to say denominations in themselves are unbiblical. Yet it does clarify that, if the Bible spoke of the *ekklesia* of Singapore, Johannesburg, or St. Louis, it would involve all of the professing Christians in the local churches in each of those cities. When the *Time* magazine article stated that 95.7 percent of Icelanders belong to a church (denominational affiliation) but only twelve percent go to church (a special edifice for worship), it makes almost no sense at all in light of the apostles' use of the term *ekklesia*.

The Body of Christ

The most extraordinary definition of the word *ekklesia* in the New Testament is the universal church, the body of Christ. The *church,* in this most innovative Christian sense, denotes the spiritual organism comprising all those who have experienced regeneration through faith in the Savior. When I place my faith in Jesus as the Son of God, who died on the cross to make me right with God, I am indwelled by the Holy Spirit and connected to Christ, the head of the church. I become part of the *ekklesia,* which is "his body" (Eph. 1:22–23; 4:15–16; Col. 1:18, 24; cf. 1 Cor. 12:12–27). Though the concept of the "body of Christ" is especially defined in Paul's writings, the concept of a universal, spiritual entity of believers is evident in many New Testament metaphors, such as "a chosen people" and "a holy nation" (1 Peter 2:9), as well as in specific teachings (Matt. 16:18; and possibly Heb. 12:28).[5]

In this sense, the universal church is the *true* and *absolute* church, incorporating all born-again believers. The apostle Peter speaks of this same universal reality: "You also, like living stones, are being built into a spiritual house to be a holy priesthood" (1 Peter 2:5). The Apocalypse opens as the Revelation of Jesus Christ, "who loves us and has freed us from our sins by his blood, and has made us to be a kingdom and priests to serve his God and Father" (Rev. 1:6). On this level, the church is a spiritual entity and does not necessarily possess formal organization. Such is the understanding of numerous theologians throughout church history. *The Westminster Confession of Faith* (1647) states: "The catholic or universal Church, which is invisible, consists of the whole number of the elect,

---

5. See K. N. Giles, "Church," in *Dictionary of the Later New Testament and Its Developments,* ed. Ralph P. Martin and Peter H. Davids (Downers Grove, Ill.: InterVarsity, 1997), 194–204; and Paul S. Minear, *Images of the Church in the New Testament* (Philadelphia: Westminster, 1960).

that have been, are, or shall be gathered into one, under Christ the head thereof."[6] Local churches belong to this invisible reality to the extent that they have members who are truly regenerate through the Holy Spirit. We may deduce that no single local church or denomination adequately reflects the fullness of the universal church, the body of Christ. This fact should keep us humble and open toward relationships with believers outside our local congregations and traditions.

These four New Testament definitions of *ekklesia* indicate that two of the most common uses of the term *church* in our society—that is, church as a *denomination* or as a *building*—are alien to the New Testament. Of course, words evolve with time, and popular uses of the term *church* are not necessarily wrong. Language changes. However, because of our preconceived notions about the church, we subconsciously tend to repack what the biblical authors were trying to communicate. Even when we clearly understand how *ekklesia* is used in the New Testament, we struggle to conceive of the *church* apart from buildings and denominational titles.

If the idea of the universal church is the overarching and ultimate meaning of *ekklesia*, we would do well to reflect on how this concept of "the body of Christ" can and should influence the forms of our local churches. In the next chapter, we will explore more fully the nature of the universal church in relation to how God has worked down through history. What is most striking is the change between Old and New Testament perspectives on how God desires to operate in and through believers.

---

6. Philip Schaff, ed., *The Westminster Confession of Faith*, 25.1, in *The Creeds of Christendom*, vol. 3, *The Evangelical and Protestant Creeds*, rev. ed. David S. Schaff, 6th ed. (reprint, Grand Rapids: Baker, 1983), 657.

Chapter 2

WHAT IS THE UNIVERSAL CHURCH?

Something immense shifted between God's way of working through political–ethical Israel in the Old Testament and the suddenly international, indeed, universal, offer of God's salvation in the New Testament. The move within the Bible from *before* to *after* the Cross is quite amazing, particularly in light of the full Jewishness of the New Testament writers, Peter, John, and Paul.

Paul, for example, prior to his conversion, was a brilliant rising star in Judaism, trained under the finest scholars and wholly engaged in defending conservative Jewish orthodoxy. He describes himself as "a Hebrew of Hebrews; in regard to the law, a Pharisee; as for zeal, persecuting the church; as for legalistic righteousness, faultless" (Phil. 3:5–6). In modern terms, Paul was a militant Jewish fundamentalist guarding the faith. Yet, after his conversion, his understanding of how God chooses to operate in the world broke his former nationalistic concepts wide open. No one in the New Testament defends God's grace more than the apostle Paul as he proclaimed the gospel among non-Jewish peoples. Jesus' death, resurrection, and the outpouring of the Holy Spirit at Pentecost changed everything. God's way of working through believers was now radically altered, and the central expression of that new way is called the church. As congregations of Christians multiplied from Jerusalem, Antioch,

Alexandria, and Ephesus, it became increasingly evident that these believers belonged to something far greater than the mere sum of local assemblies. Above the local gatherings and geographic clusters of churches, a transcendent, unifying image of the church was emerging, whose head is Christ.

What constitutes the universal church, and how does it compare with Old Testament Israel? Healthy debate and dialogue are happening among Christians of varying traditions about the nature of the universal church. These differences carry practical implications for one's ecclesiology that go far beyond denominational differences. Such distinctions serve as compasses that guide our understanding of nearly everything we do as the body of Christ. All agree that there are continuities and discontinuities between the Old and New Testaments regarding the way in which the kingdom of God operated through Israel and, subsequently, through the Christian church. The following considerations are foundational for a solid and practical ecclesiology for the local church today.

Unity and Diversity in Salvation History

Many theologians in historical Christianity have interpreted the church as the community of all believers in all times, from Adam and Eve to Noah, Abraham, and Moses, on through Christ and the apostles to the end of time. Such a deduction makes a lot of sense, for it is only through Christ's death on the cross that a person is made right or justified before God. This is true whether in the Old Testament through anticipatory faith in God's promises, or later, in the New Testament, through faith in the Son of God and his atonement at Calvary. In every era of the history of salvation, mankind is saved through faith in the Living God. Obviously, then, various parallels exist between the people of God in the Old Testament and those in the New.

On the other hand, along with the similarities among the people of God, all admit some differences in the manner in which God has revealed himself and what he asks of those who believe. For example, whereas clear mandates are given in the Old Testament about animal sacrifices, Christians do not offer sacrifices in a tabernacle or temple in Jerusalem. Neither do we keep the actual Sabbath of the fourth commandment (Ex.

20:8–11), which is Saturday. We do not stone to death adulterers or disrespectful children. In contrast to Joshua when he entered the Promised Land, we do not march to war to annihilate our enemies in the name of the Lord. Rather, the Bible itself shows that God's revelation progresses through history, fulfilling, completing, and leaving some aspects behind while revealing other elements for the future.

Thus, there is unity and diversity, continuity and discontinuity, between the ways in which God works down through history. Some theologians emphasize the *sameness;* others accentuate the radical differences.[1] In the following two sections, I will suggest several reasons for affirming qualified and necessary distinctions between believing Israel in the Old Testament and Christian believers in the New Testament. Moreover, these distinctions make all the difference for the practical life of the local church for reasons that will unfold in the following chapters.

The Church, a New Reality: Theological Arguments

The Incarnation and the Unforeseen Gospel

Few would question that the Old Testament speaks of a growing hope for a messiah, regardless of how "the Coming One" might have been interpreted among intertestamental Jews. Nevertheless, virtually no biblical scholar today would admit that Old Testament believers comprehended the kind of Christ we see in the Gospels—even though, retrospectively, many elements of Jesus' coming can be perceived in the Old Testament from a New Testament vantage. The unique revelation in Jesus Christ caught everyone by surprise. In *what* and in *whom* one believed changed substantially with the Incarnation, the life and teaching of Jesus, the Cross, Resurrection, and Ascension. Although Noah, Abraham, Moses, David, and Daniel trusted in the Lord—the same covenantal God manifested in the

---

1. Presentations of arguments for and against identifying Israel and the church are found in John S. Feinberg, ed., *Continuity and Discontinuity: Perspectives on the Relationship Between the Old and New Testaments; Essays in Honor of S. Lewis Johnson Jr.* (Wheaton, Ill.: Crossway, 1988); and Craig A. Blaising and Darrell L. Bock, eds., *Dispensationalism, Israel and the Church: The Search for Definition* (Grand Rapids: Zondervan, 1992).

New Testament—they had no clear sense that this same God is a Holy Trinity or that the Son of God would assume human nature and by his brutal crucifixion redeem the world. This is to say, one reason for affirming discontinuity between the Old and New Testaments is that what believers *believe* shifted significantly between the faithful of Judaism and the Christian church. The content of Christian faith centers in the incarnate Son of God and his death and resurrection, which the faithful saints in the Old Testament seem not to have foreknown.

Mystery and the Church

Similarly, Paul speaks plainly of the new revelation given by the Holy Spirit: "The *mystery* made known to me . . . the mystery of Christ, which was not made known to men in other generations as it has now been revealed by the Spirit to God's holy apostles and prophets" (Eph. 3:3–5, italics added). He continues, "This mystery, which for ages past was kept hidden in God . . . [so that] through the church, the manifold wisdom of God should be made known" (Eph. 3:9–10; see 1:9–10). In other words, God's grace now finds innovative, surprising provision for the non-Jewish world in the church. Through the Cross, Gentile believers are united with Jewish Christians as "members together of one body, and sharers together in the promise in Christ Jesus" (Eph. 3:6). Thus, not only are the Incarnation and the Cross new revelations in which we are called to believe, but the universal church itself also constitutes God's previously undisclosed mystery, a new theology, a new-sprung reality of his creative working.

One Kingdom, Distinct Expressions

As in various other passages, the words of Jesus in Matthew 11:11 seem difficult to understand if there is not a categorical shift between believers under the old covenant and those under the new. John the Baptist is, in a sense, the last of the great Old Testament prophets (11:13), but Jesus inaugurates something far superior: "I tell you the truth: Among those born of women there has not risen anyone greater than John the Baptist; yet *he who is least in the kingdom of heaven is greater than he*" (italics added). Now, in one sense, the kingdom of heaven (or "kingdom of God," as in Luke 7:28) was already present in the Old Testament and up until John the Baptist, because the kingdom of God is wherever God rules. But in another sense, a new form of God's rule was being inaugurated in Jesus Christ, one that was superior to all that had occurred before, including the ministry of John the Baptist.[2] In the kingdom now announced by Jesus, the position of even the least honorable member was more privileged than that of the greatest person of faith under the old order. In other words, the disciples (as are you and I today) are privy to and privileged with something that John the Baptist was not. I think it is fair to deduce that in one sense, *one kingdom* of God unites the two Testaments in the whole of salvation history. But, in another sense, the form and promises of the kingdom inaugurated by Jesus Christ and put into effect by the Holy Spirit at Pentecost changed significantly from that which was earlier revealed to Old Testament Israel down through John the Baptist. In later chapters, we will return to this theme of the remarkable change in the form of God's kingdom between Israel and Christ's church.

One People, Different Conditions of Faith

Just as the one kingdom of God is expressed in progressive, particular ways, so there exists *one people of God* united through trusting God but distinguished by what God sets forth as faith's conditions. The phrase "people of God" and its parallels are employed frequently to describe Israel in the Old Testament (Judg. 20:2; 2 Sam. 14:13), and just as clearly to describe the church in the New Testament. The author of Hebrews includes Old and New Testament saints together in the "people of God" (Heb. 4:9). The apostle Peter writes to Christians, "Now you are the people of God" (1 Peter 2:10), and Paul declares that Gentile believers are now "fellow citizens with God's people and members of God's household" (Eph.

---

2. Various leading commentaries concur that Jesus here speaks of a new elevated order, superior to all that has occurred prior to the Savior. Among others, see Eduard Schweizer, *The Good News According to Matthew*, trans. David E. Green (London: SPCK, 1976), 261; Robert H. Mounce, *Matthew* (San Francisco: Harper and Row, 1985), 103; and W. F. Albright and C. S. Mann, *Matthew*, Anchor Bible Commentary (New York: Doubleday, 1971), 137.

2:19).[3] The opinion of many is that the church exists as part of the larger community of God's people. That is, the "people of God" includes subgroups down through biblical history, each reflecting its uniqueness while also standing accepted through faith in what God has revealed. From one perspective, we might say that all subgroups of believers down through history belong to the same condominium, but each has its own apartment with distinct family rules. Of course, some conditions for living in the condominium appear fairly much the same, as they reflect the character of the Owner. Other conditions are unique to each subgroup, in the discretion and wisdom of the Owner, who allows each to enter through his grace.

That unity and diversity mark God's people should not seem strange, given the infinite creativity of our God. Interestingly, even angels are called "sons of God" (Job 1:6; 2:1, footnotes), "the holy ones [saints]" of God (Zech. 14:5; cf. Matt. 25:31), and "the *assembly* of the holy ones [saints]" (Ps. 89:5, 7). But no one would say that angels are part of Israel or part of the church in the New Testament sense of *ekklesia*. The hosts of angels are part of a greater worshiping community in the presence of God the Father and Jesus Christ (Heb. 12:22–23; Rev. 5:11–13). In heaven they too sing, "Worthy is the Lamb, who was slain." But angels do not belong to the church any more than Israel belongs to the church or the church to Israel. Surely we are heirs of Abraham by faith. We are one people with the Old Testament saints, and one of an even larger number who worship the true God revealed in Jesus Christ. But the divine conditions of faith and service for the members of God's community are expressed in some ways quite differently.

The Tri-Unity of God

In Christianity, we worship *one* God. But this God reveals himself as three persons: Father, Son, and Holy Spirit. The eternal God exists in the mystery of tri-unity. In the creative work of God, the tendency is not toward simplicity but toward extraordinary complexity, yet all within a

---

3. The New Testament phrase translated in the *Holy Bible,* New International Version, as "God's people" (nine times) usually and more literally reads "saints" or "holy ones" (Gk *hagios*). It often refers to Christian believers (Rom. 12:13; 1 Cor. 16:1; 2 Cor. 9:12; Eph. 3:8; 4:12; Heb. 13:24). For example, the NIV renders the final verse of the Bible, "The grace of the Lord Jesus be with *God's people.* Amen" (Rev. 22:21, italics added).

harmony of reality. In other words, all creation flows forth from and is reflective of who God is as Holy Trinity. Appropriate to the very being of the Godhead, signs of both oneness and many-ness are manifest in virtually every divine creation, whether in the physical world or in the spiritual dimensions. The structure of all created existence flows forth from the triune Artist's own personal reality. As we have seen, the same unity and diversity are apparent within the believing community down through time. In describing the distinctions between Israel and the church, the apostle Paul cries out, "Oh, the depth of the riches of the wisdom and knowledge of God! How unsearchable his judgments, and his paths beyond tracing out!" (Rom. 11:33). The diversity among the people of God—as between Israel and the church—reflects something of the mysterious oneness and threeness of the Trinity itself.

In summary, five theological reasons persuade one that the church constitutes a new reality distinct from Israel:

1. The content of truly Christian faith centers in the incarnate Son and the gospel, of which those in the Old Testament had little if any knowledge.
2. Paul declares "the mystery of Christ," veiled to saints in the past, that now conjoins all who believe in Jesus Christ—Jews and Gentiles alike—into one body, the church.
3. Although one kingdom of God finally unites the two Testaments, the forms of the kingdom assume markedly different expressions according to the purposes of God.
4. All true believers are heirs of Abraham and "one people," yet God has distinguished certain "familial" conditions and promises for the church that are not identical to those of Old Testament Israel.
5. Because God is Trinity, distinctions among God's people should not surprise us; it is God's nature to reveal personal unity in diversity and diversity in unity.

The Church and Pentecost: An Exegetical Argument

As mentioned previously, much has been written regarding similarities and dissimilarities between the Testaments, and ours is but a very brief survey. Yet one other particularly strong set of textual evidences should be set forth that appear to mandate the conclusion that the *church* is not a synonym for *Israel*. Rather, the Christian church begins specifically at Pentecost.[4] Four simple sets of biblical data lead to this verdict: Jesus spoke of the church as future; Jesus spoke of Spirit baptism as future; the baptism of the Holy Spirit began at Pentecost, marking every member of the body of Christ; and "the body of Christ" *is* the church.

Jesus Spoke of the Church as Future

"I will build my church" (Matt. 16:18). Though *ekklesia* might elsewhere include a more general meaning of "assembly," in Matthew 16:18, Jesus speaks of "my church" and he speaks of it as *future*. If Jesus spoke in Aramaic (which is probable), then Matthew's Greek translation all the more denotes the *Christian* church to which the evangelist was writing. Built on the disciple Peter's confession that Jesus is "the Christ, the Son of the living God," the church was perceived by its own Savior as yet to be constructed. For that reason, the Lord Jesus is the cornerstone (Eph. 2:20; 1 Peter 2:6), the first block by which all else is aligned.

Jesus Spoke of Spirit Baptism as Future

Our Lord also spoke of the baptism of the Holy Spirit as yet to occur. Only hours before his crucifixion, Jesus promised "another Counselor," one who had been until this point *with* the disciples but who soon would be *in* them (John 14:16–17). Following the Resurrection, and moments before his ascension into heaven, the Lord Jesus declared: "For John baptized with water, but in a few days you *will be baptized* with the Holy Spirit" (Acts 1:5, italics added). Ten days later at the Feast of Pentecost, this promised baptism of the Holy Spirit occurred (Acts 2:1–4). Although the Spirit surely came upon prophets and others in the Old Testament, the special reality of the baptism of the Holy Spirit apparently had never happened prior to the events depicted in Acts 2. This constitutes a new phase of God's working. Several years after Pentecost, in discussing the

---

4. I am indebted to Charles Ryrie for this chronology of argument.

nature of the church with his fellow apostles, Peter referred to that first baptism of the Holy Spirit as "the beginning" and the direct fulfillment of Christ's promise (Acts 11:15–16). We have observed, then, that Jesus, during his earthly ministry, referred to both the church and the baptism of the Holy Spirit as *future*; whereas, Peter proclaims "the beginning" and the baptism of the Spirit as *past*, having already begun at Pentecost.

Spirit Baptism and the Body of Christ

The baptism and indwelling of the Holy Spirit mark every member of the body of Christ. The apostle Paul's normative teaching is found in 1 Corinthians 12:13: "For *we were all baptized by one Spirit into one body*— whether Jews or Greeks, slave or free—and we were all given one Spirit to drink" (italics added). Whatever doctrinal differences might relate to this matter, one thing is clear in the text: If a person is not baptized in the Holy Spirit, then he or she is not part of the body of Christ. The baptism of the Holy Spirit is the spiritual miracle that places a believer into the body of Christ. At the moment of belief, a real union occurs between the new Christian and Jesus Christ when the Holy Spirit inhabits the believer. The indwelling of the Holy Spirit also begins to fulfill Old Testament prophetic promises to Israel (Jer. 31:33; Heb. 8:8–12; see Matt. 3:11), yet this indwelling serves especially as "a seal" and "a deposit guaranteeing [every Christian's] inheritance" (Eph. 1:13–14). Although the disciples in the upper room at Pentecost were *filled* with the Spirit, anointed with great boldness, and spoke in tongues, the Spirit's *baptism* itself is theologically a distinct reality—as Paul clarifies to his readers in Corinth.[5] Not identical to filling and fullness, the baptism of the Holy Spirit brings every true Christian into a kind of organic oneness with both the Head

---

5. Gordon Fee, *God's Empowering Presence: The Holy Spirit in the Letters of Paul* (Peabody, Mass.: Hendrickson, 1994), 180–81. Fee, a Pentecostal scholar, admits that baptism appears very much the "common experience of conversion." Fee adds that there is no clear statement in Paul where baptism is a second experience. Moreover, from my own vantage, if the baptism of the Spirit were a second sanctifying experience, then of all the churches of the New Testament, Paul should have exhorted the Corinthians (plagued by carnality) to seek the higher ground of the baptism of the Spirit. To the contrary, Paul presumes that those in the Corinthian church already were baptized in the Spirit (1 Cor. 12:13).

of the body and the other members of the invisible body of Christ. That is, whatever else might accompany the baptism of the Spirit, the phrase itself defines the believer's immersion or joining into the spiritual body of Christ, the universal church. For this reason, whether in Belarus or Mongolia, whether separated by tribal languages in Venezuela or by Arabic and ethnic dialects in Khartoum, Christians enjoy a genuine unity, a fellowship, that transcends all nationalities and differences. Spirit baptism is an essential and distinguishing mark of all true Christians; it sets us apart from believers prior to Pentecost and joins us with Jesus Christ and with one another today.

The Body of Christ Is the Church

Finally, the New Testament identifies the body of Christ as the church and the church as the body of Christ: "He is the head of the body, the church" (Col. 1:18); "his body, which is the church" (1:24); "the church, which is his body" (Eph. 1:22–23; see 4:15–16; 1 Cor. 12:12–27). That Paul employs the two terms as synonymous is undeniable.

How does it add together? While on earth, Jesus spoke of the church as future. He also foretold the baptism of the Holy Spirit. The baptism of the Spirit occurred at Pentecost. And Paul teaches that only those baptized in the Holy Spirit belong to the body of Christ, which is the church. It's short math to figure out that the church could have begun only at Pentecost. Whether universal or local in its meaning, the *ekklesia* of the New Testament is different from Israel and has certain characteristics that distinguish it from other ways of God's working.

So the church was born out of Israel, but it is not Israel. At the same time, everyone admits that the book of Acts describes a transition period when not everything fit into neat categories. Certainly, characteristics from the Old Testament carry over into the New Testament. For example, the outpouring of the Spirit and the abundance of God's grace to the nations both fulfill Old Testament prophecies and reflect a greater future reality when Christ returns. One might even interpret the baptism of the Spirit as the return of God's glory to a new temple—a temple now built of believers in Jesus Christ rather than on Herod's massive stone foundations. But the church, the universal church, is a *new* creation, a *mystery* previously unrevealed. The consequences of such a conclusion for the local church may surprise you.

At this point, we have traveled through quite a lot of countryside. You may be on board with the theological and biblical arguments, or you may be hanging on the rails. You need not entirely agree. Anyone who admits significant divergences between the way believers were called to obey God in the Old Testament versus the New Testament should consider further what those differences might mean. If we take the New Testament seriously, the implications of these differences are substantial regarding the way we "do church." Somewhere along the line, we have lost our ecclesiological map, and for that reason a lot of our churches are in trouble as we enter the twenty-first century. Our challenge in the coming decades is not necessarily to grow bigger or even to maintain what we have—although these may be worthy objectives. Rather, our challenge is to better *be* the church that Christ desires. How our ecclesiology has lost its way is the subject of the next chapter.

Chapter 3

CENTERED IN CHRIST, DECENTRALIZED IN THE WORLD

The New Testament distinction of the church from Israel is important for how we understand the *ekklesia* of the first centuries *and* the twenty-first century. The differences include far-reaching principles for the activities and structures of the local church. If Pentecost represents a new work of God in history, then we might expect certain dissimilarities between the form of the kingdom of God in the Old Testament and that in the New Testament. Indeed, the transition from a *centralized* expression of God's will through Israel to a *decentralized* form through the body of Christ is categorical. For the earliest believers, consisting primarily of Jewish Christians, the new reality of the church as it was emerging for example at the Jerusalem Council in Acts 15 was nothing less than astounding.

Israel's Centralized Kingdom

The dominant paradigm of God's working in the Old Testament was through Israel with all its ethnic, geographical, temporal, and religious particularities. The Jewish people were the hub of God's revelation and call to salvation among the nations. The Old Testament expression of the kingdom of God especially centered on four realms.

Race

In the Hebrew Scriptures, through God's covenant with Abraham (Gen. 12:1–3; 15:4–22; 17:3–8, 15–19; 22:15–18), salvation was understood to be through the Jews. If the kingdom of God was universal in Adam and Noah, with Father Abraham it becomes focused in the Hebrew race. God's "chosen people" were the Israelites, the descendants of Abraham, Isaac, and Jacob. Indeed, because of foreign idolatry, to marry outside the race was strictly prohibited (Deut. 7:3; 1 Kings 11:1–2). Thus began an ethnic, racial center to the Lord's working in the world: salvation is through the Jewish people.

Place

Second, with the establishment of Israel's monarchy through David and Solomon, worship and service to God were oriented geographically to Israel and Jerusalem. Gentile nations were called to recognize Israel as God's regent and mediator on the earth. To worship the true God, non-Jewish people were called to bring offerings to Jerusalem and more specifically to the temple (1 Chron. 16:28–29; Ps. 96:7–8). Yet, Gentile visitors were prohibited beyond the outer court (later the Court of the Gentiles) from closer proximity to the Lord God. Likewise, the Israelites themselves were constrained by tiers of regulations in drawing closer to God. Each version of the temple, from Solomon to Herod, distinguished limits between laity and priests. Herod's temple provided a Court of Women, then a Court of Men. Each temple construction included an inner sanctuary for priests and, finally, the highly restricted Holy of Holies. We see that the locus of the kingdom of God in the physical world was spatially and territorially defined and tightly regulated. Worship was centered in a geography—the City of Zion, the temple, and the Holy of Holies.

Time

Third, God set apart for Israel special days, religious holidays and the Sabbath. Mandated Old Testament feasts included Passover, Unleavened Bread, Firstfruits, Weeks (Pentecost), Trumpets (Rosh Hashanah—New

Year's Day), the Day of Atonement (Yom Kippur), Tabernacles (Booths), and others. Even more importantly in the giving of the Mosaic Law, the Lord God established the Sabbath. As the fourth commandment, keeping the Sabbath served as one of two visible covenantal signs—the other being circumcision—that set Israel apart from the nations (Ex. 20:8–12; 31:12–17). Interestingly, no evidence exists that any human being, anywhere, practiced any kind of Sabbath until God began to orient Israel with the falling of the manna in the wilderness (Ex. 16:23–30).[1] Contrary to some who insist the Sabbath has always been a biblical command, Nehemiah reminds postexilic Judah that God made known to them the Sabbath at Mount Sinai (Neh. 9:14; see Ezek. 20:12–21). While all Jews were to love the Lord God with all their hearts and all the time, there was a temporal focus to Israel's worship: mandated religious festivals, and especially the seventh day of the week—Saturday, the Sabbath.

Priesthood

Fourth, the high priest and a hierarchy of Levitical priests functioned as mediators between God and humanity. The tribe of Levi served as experts and professionals regarding the ceremonies and sacrifices of the Mosaic Law. Whether on behalf of Israel or of the nations, all religious ceremony passed through them. Circumventing their priesthood, as King Saul did by offering his own sacrifice (1 Sam. 13:8–14), incurred the judgment of God. The Levites were a family hierarchy, a clan, a tribe, a self-propagating religious caste. Obviously, the Lord God himself designated

---

1. Though the words are related, the Hebrew term *sabbath* is not the same as "seventh day" in Genesis 2:2–3. Unlike the practice of circumcision, which was sometimes found among other nations, there is no historical precedent to worship on the Sabbath among either the Old Testament patriarchs or the non-Jewish nations. The term is first mentioned in Exodus 16:22–30 and again in 20:8–11 (the Decalogue). Given the long explanations in both texts, the impression is that the concept of Sabbath was unfamiliar to the Israelites (see 20:22). Of the Ten Commandments, the fourth is the longest and the only one with extensive directions, longer than commandments five through ten combined. Among all the nations, only Israel was held accountable for keeping the Sabbath. This is not to deny the need for rest before the Lord as an ongoing principle.

the Levites as priests. And he commanded them to administer the Law of his kingdom in and through Israel.

Thus, in an indisputably marked way, the Old Testament manner of worship and service to God was by very nature *centralized*. It was centralized *racially* in the Jews. It was centralized *geographically* in Israel, Jerusalem, the temple, and the Holy of Holies. It was centralized *temporally* in the Sabbath and certain religious holidays. And it was centralized in a *religious hierarchy* of priests, without whom it was illicit even to offer sacrifices.

For the Israelites, the *external* was the concretization of the *internal*. Physical realities were the vivid means for expressing faith and worship to the Lord God. External benefits—such as rainfall, plentiful harvests, many children, and rest from war—were God's means of spiritually blessing his people. Conversely, God's physical curses and punishments forcefully reminded Israel of their waywardness from him. Old Testament commands even circumscribed Israel's political and economic realities. In all this, we must never forget that it is the Lord God himself who prescribed these forms of national worship and behavior—and these in great detail. Obedience to the Law of Moses and the word of the prophets is what Yahweh required.

The Decentralized Kingdom of the Church

When we look at the church of Jesus Christ in the New Testament, we discover an extraordinary inversion of the old form of God's working in the world.

The People

Rather than being centralized racially in the Jews, the church is a *universal* and *spiritual* entity designed for all people, without discrimination or ethnic preference. While not denying Old Testament promises to the nation of Israel, the church emerges as a *new* chosen people, a *new* holy nation belonging to God (1 Peter 2:9). Indeed, far above what was offered in the Old Testament, every Christian is given direct filial relationship with God by adoption through Christ. We are sons and daughters of the One whom Jesus invites us to call our Father. Male or female, regardless of age, race, or station in life, every believer in Christ is considered a legitimate heir of God the Father (Gal. 3:26–4:7). The communitarian emphasis on the Jewish nation has shifted to the Christian proclamation of every individual's need for personal faith in Jesus Christ regardless of nationality or culture. Each believing Christian is equally heir of the Most High God. Because of the strong promises through the Cross for all who believe, God has no favorites in terms of race, age, or gender. Like the two hundred-foot outstretched arms of Christ at Rio Janeiro's Corcovado, God's grace extends to all. No longer centralized in a select nation, regenerate individuals are the agents and mediators of the kingdom of God and together form the church of Jesus Christ.

The Place

In the Hebrew Testament, as we have seen above, the nations are repeatedly invited to pilgrimage to Jerusalem and bring offerings to the temple. The nations are to *come* to Zion. Conversely, in the New Testament, Christ's departing words are to *go into all the world* (Matt. 28:19). Rather than being called to centralize geographically in Israel, Jerusalem, and the temple, Christians were sent *from* Jerusalem into all Judea, Samaria, and the ends of the world (Acts 1:8).

The following chart illustrates the geographic centralization of the Old Testament kingdom from the nations to the pinnacle-center of God's presence in the Holy of Holies; whereas, after the Cross, the church is sent forth from its center in Jerusalem to the uttermost parts of the earth. (This dialectic of biblical history between Israel and the church does not include other realities in the history of salvation, whether before Old Testament Israel or after the New Testament church.)

In the church, worship and service to God are no longer oriented to a temple. There is no longer a "house of God"—no sanctuary, no altar, no Holy of Holies. Nor, today, are believers' worship and service to God centralized in a local church's building or in real estate. We often overlook that early Christian communities had no special buildings, temples, or sanctuaries for meetings. Believers met wherever they could—in homes, Jewish synagogues, catacombs, forests, or desert ravines. Geography no longer mattered. Historically, the earliest edifices clearly identified as

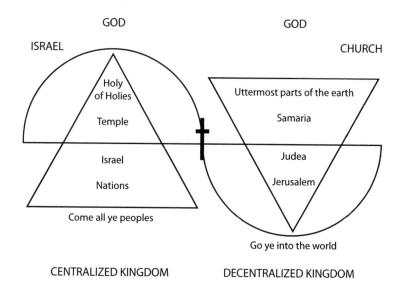

public Christian places of worship date from the late third century, almost 250 years after the death of Christ. Rather than focus their resources and activities in buildings, the early church understood that in the body of Christ, geography is no longer important. Where there is *one* Christian, or where two or three come together, *there* exists the real temple of God. The body of Christ, the invisible church, is the true temple of the Living God (1 Cor. 3:9, 16–17; 6:19; 1 Peter 2:5–7). Local churches are meant to be the expression of that powerful reality. As the chosen race is now composed of elect individuals, so the center of God's geography is no longer Jerusalem but everywhere his people love and serve him—and that in local churches all over the planet.

The Day

Jewish worship centralized temporally in the Sabbath and special feasts and celebrations. The Christian faith has no such command, though Christians might well appreciate celebrations at Christmas and Easter. The New Testament church, for example, has no Yom Kippur or any other mandated "holy day." Early on, the apostolic leadership of the church was confronted with the question of what parts of the Mosaic Law non-Jewish converts were to keep (Acts 15:1–31). Although they themselves were unanimously Jewish, James and the Jerusalem Council concluded, "It seemed good to the Holy Spirit and to us not to burden you [the Gentile believers and churches] with anything beyond . . . [a very few] requirements" (v. 28). Significantly, given the importance of the Sabbath in Judaism, the Jerusalem Council omitted any reference whatsoever to setting apart Saturday or Sunday as holy days for non-Jewish believers.

Why might that be? In the Bible, circumcision and the Sabbath—the two outward signs of God's covenant with Israel—appear to be replaced by two new commands for the church: water baptism and the Lord's Supper (Matt. 28:19; 1 Cor. 11:23–26). Similar to circumcision, baptism is a once-for-all induction into the covenantal community. Similar to the Sabbath, the Eucharist (or Communion) repeatedly calls the local church to remember her Savior's atoning death and Second Coming. Baptism is once and for all and the Lord's Supper is a regular, ongoing act of worship and covenant remembrance.

Surely in some cultures, historical and pragmatic reasons exist to observe Sunday as a special day of worship. It is the day of our Savior's resurrection, with the wonder and joy marking that occasion. On "the first day of the week," Paul preached late into the night before leaving the Ephesian believers (Acts 20:7). On Sunday, "every week," the Corinthian believers were to set aside money for offerings (1 Cor. 16:2), a probable occasion for the church to gather. John's Revelation of Jesus Christ came "on the Lord's Day," the only occurrence of the phrase in the New Testament (Rev. 1:10). From the earliest post-apostolic records, Sunday has been a common day of Christian assembly.[2]

On the other hand, the scant biblical references to Sunday are descriptive, *not* prescriptive. No New Testament teachings justify applying the fourth commandment of "keeping the Sabbath" to Sunday or any day of Christian worship. One might properly wonder how Peter, Paul, and the other apostles understood Sunday. Today's form of God's activity in the world appears to

---

2. Ignatius *Epistle to the Magnesians*, 9:1 (c. A.D. 108); *Didache*, 14:1 (c. 115); *Epistle of Barnabas*, 15:9 (c. 130).

allow believing communities the freedom to choose when to worship. In some cultures, Christians gather at daybreak, others at noon. Latin Americans often prefer the evenings. Employment in secular culture often pressures believers to work on Sunday, yet permits other days of rest. Various contemporary local churches find that Saturday or Wednesday gatherings can best meet the needs of at least some of their members for fellowship and worship. Christians in Muslim cultures where repression is severe might sometimes choose Friday, the Islamic holy day, as their own—indeed, it is the day of Jesus' sacrifice and our redemption. In short, the New Testament mandate is that we "not give up meeting together" so that we "may spur one another on toward love and good deeds" and "encourage one another" (Heb. 10:24–25). Though we may admire the conviction of the Olympic runner Eric Liddell in *Chariots of Fire,* Romans 14:5 reminds us that "one man considers one day more sacred than another; another man considers every day alike. Each one should be fully convinced in his own mind." (See also Gal. 4:8–11; Col. 2:16–17.) Such convictions do not atomize a congregation, so that everyone ends up doing his or her own thing. Rather, options regarding the times of coming together should be determined in light of the collective needs of the local believers. Christian leaders in the twenty-first century have an opportunity to bring believers together "in church" through innovative forms, rather than generate guilt for not meeting on Sunday.

In all this, the Lord's people are dependent on the Holy Spirit, the Spirit of wisdom and grace. Although the New Testament is open regarding times of congregational worship, I think it important to affirm that Sunday is the *preferred* day of worship, both from the biblical pattern and the long tradition of Christian history. Indeed, in some contexts, Sunday worship serves as a form of Christian testimony to unbelieving observers. So the mix of New Testament freedom together with cultural patterns, Christian heritage, and local needs resists simplistic solutions or facile changes for the sake of novelty. Yet the point remains: So long as we are committed regularly to joining with other believers in the local church, there appears to be liberty regarding the choice of day and time. No day is prescribed *or* proscribed. The New Testament assembly has biblical freedom to determine the best times for worship.

The Clergy

Finally, rather than centralize in a professional religious hierarchy like the Levites, each Christian is declared a priest with direct access to God the Father through Jesus Christ (1 Peter 2:5). Jesus "made us to be a kingdom and priests to serve his God and Father" (Rev. 1:6). The New Testament, of course, affirms the necessity of qualified leadership in the church through bishops, overseers, presbyters, elders, and pastors (which appear as essentially synonymous, cf. Acts 20:17, 28; 1 Peter 5:1–4). Deacons are a secondary level of leadership, and some would add deaconesses as well (1 Tim. 3:8–12). However, Christian leadership is not a professional caste as in the Old Testament. Though a pastor must be "*a* man of God," he is not "*the* man of God," the sole prophet and mediator for a congregation. He does not assume a position of CEO or executive or high priest. Christian leaders do not funnel all the efforts and resources of the congregation to their particular plans for ministry and expansion. Rather, they are under-shepherds to the Great Shepherd.[3] New Testament leadership has been given to the body of Christ in order to perfect each member into the image and fullness of Christ in this world (Eph. 4:11–16). Rather than create dependency on themselves, biblical leaders teach others to hear and to obey Jesus Christ as the true Head of the church—to do what Christ would do in the world, to be salt and light wherever they are. True biblical leadership *equips* and *frees* believers to serve the Lord in the diverse activities of life.

Moreover, although Christian leaders are first responsible for the strengthening of the local church, this is never to the exclusion of helping other believers, whatever their denomination may be. New Testament

---

3. In the New Testament, the term *pastor* is usually a functional term, denoting activity in relation to the congregation. Therefore, women, too, as equals before God, may have pastoral roles and even the office of pastor in a qualified sense. But as reflective of Trinitarian order, ecclesial order seems to include ultimate male leadership, as in the home. Neither equality before God nor commands for reciprocal self-giving undo the New Testament mandates for order and responsibility. These are rooted not only in specific situations and ancient culture, but also in relation to the Godhead, angels, the order of creation, and the order of the fall (1 Cor. 11:3, 10; 1 Tim. 2:11–14). Nevertheless, Scripture also suggests a certain flexibility in how Trinitarian order and equality are applied in different cultural and local situations.

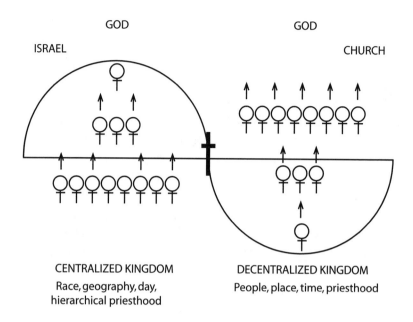

CENTRALIZED KINGDOM
Race, geography, day,
hierarchical priesthood

DECENTRALIZED KINGDOM
People, place, time, priesthood

leaders build and nurture the body of Christ in whatever circumstances. Though a pastor may have a specific flock to shepherd, he has no right to restrict his ministry to a closed circle of denominational or local church members.

Therefore, in contrast to the Old Testament form of the kingdom of God, the New Testament church is an organism centralized in Jesus Christ and characterized by a decentralized vision for ministry in the world. The church is called to penetrate the world with the message and love of Christ. Rather than existing for itself, it is called to diffuse into the world as Christ's body. The church serves as Christ's feet and hands, ears and mouth wherever most needed.

In short, race, geography (buildings), days and times, and even clergy are finally peripheral to the central purposes of the church.

Theory versus Reality

But does this decentralized New Testament form of the kingdom characterize the believing church today? Are local church activities equipping saints to live out Christ in the world? to live daily with ears attuned to the will of the Lord Jesus and the direction of the Holy Spirit in the marketplace? Or could it be that many of us are in great part preoccupied with our programs, administration, and building maintenance? When our image of the church is *popular* rather than *biblical*, it is easy to concern ourselves with appearance, hierarchy, and income. In the words of Gibson Winter, ecclesial analyst of nearly a half-century ago, "The introverted church is one which puts its own survival before its mission, its own identity above its task, its internal concerns before its apostolate, its rituals before its ministry."[5] Church activities can drain the spiritual energy of a congregation rather than impelling members into significant engagement with a lost world. We regress into equating performances, committees, buildings, and budgets with the *ministry* of the body of Christ.

As a young pastor, I found there was always more to do around a church. I straightened chairs and picked up bulletins. I cleaned the flower beds and dusted cobwebs. I began to realize that I could *live* in the church, preparing messages and bulletins, arranging worship, organizing meetings, and administering committees. My inexperience led me to assume that emotional music, careful exposition, and aggressively orchestrated programs made for a successful and spiritually vibrant church. I could not, however, escape troubling doubts that this was not the way it was supposed to be. Preconceptions of what successful churches should be like and how pastors should work are subtle yet overwhelming. The assumptions are shared by pastors and members alike. As Christian leaders strive to replicate what members have come to expect (and what we expect of ourselves), we can often lose our centeredness in the Lord. Our *reason for being* as individuals and as a church gives way to our own narcissistic desires for growth and success. Not that a church should pride itself in undynamic music or a pastor in ineloquent preaching! But our obsession with appearance and performance can replace what the New Testament church was all about. The recent proliferation of nontraditional

5. Gibson Winter, *The Suburban Captivity of the Churches: An Analysis of Protestant Responsibility in the Expanding Metropolis* (Garden City, N.Y.: Doubleday, 1961), 120.

Christian gatherings—often Gen-X (or Y)—whether in North Atlantic countries or around the world, indicates an increasing disillusionment with the church as big business.

Of course no local church will be ideal. In mid-2004, of the nearly 2.1 billion people who profess Christian faith worldwide, the actual number of "church attenders" totals just over 1.4 billion. These divide into nearly 3,663,00 congregations (or "worship centers"), representing some 37,000 different denominations plus thousands of independent works.[6] All churches express the traditions, cultures, and inclinations of their membership and leaders. Much of this plurality is healthy, so long as sound doctrine, righteousness, and open-handedness with others reflect the triune God's character and will. Yet a study of the New Testament suggests that many of today's forms and structures of the local church may actually *hinder* the true work of God in the world.

Ecclesial methods that drain rather than disseminate the members' energy contradict the decentralizing direction of the New Testament form of the kingdom of God. Far too many churches today perpetuate little more than formalities and forms. Far too many Christian workers have been domesticated and chained, willingly or not, to ecclesiological systems that detract from the fulfillment of the divine call on their lives and undermine God's mandate for the church.

How the church turned inward on itself rather than continuing to pursue Christ's outward mandate will be the topic of our next chapter.

---

6. David B. Barrett and Todd M. Johnson, "Annual Statistical Table on Global Mission: 2004," *International Bulletin of Missionary Research* 28, no. 1 (January 2004), 25. This data builds on David B. Barrett et al., eds., *World Christian Encyclopedia: A Comparative Survey of Churches and Religions in the Modern World*, 2 vols., 2d ed. (Oxford: Oxford University Press, 2001).

Chapter 4

WHAT HAPPENED?

AN ABBREVIATED TOUR
THROUGH CHURCH HISTORY

Why does the Christian church today place so much emphasis on matters that the early church did not? How did the church come to redefine itself around buildings, Sunday gatherings, the worship service (as liturgy and/or performance), and professional clergy? Though much has been written about the history of the early church, this is not a simple question to answer.

Early Organization

The earliest Christian believers were Jewish. Jesus taught in the synagogues, the newborn church met daily in the temple courts to pray (Acts 2:46), and as the apostles and evangelists disseminated from Jerusalem, their most receptive audience were those steeped in the Old Testament in Jewish synagogues around the Roman Empire. Although the church increasingly was weaned from Judaism, the structure of the church naturally reflected the organizational form of the synagogues, with elders and itinerate teachers—even as elements of Roman civil organization also became apparent. Along with the apostles, others were soon selected to help *serve* (lit. "wait on") the growing community (Acts 6:1–7). Certainly *deacons* such as Philip and Stephen excelled as evangelists themselves. Tacitus, in his *Annals*, attests to the rapid growth of the church when he writes of Nero's persecution in A.D. 64 of "a massive crowd" *(multido ingens)* of Christian believers in Rome.[1] Through the New Testament, we observe organizational growth regarding the offices of elder and deacon, although more is required of their character than is specified in terms of their service (1 Tim. 3:1–10; Titus 1:5–9). And though structures of church governance are occasionally evident, little is actually prescribed beyond the requirements for qualified leadership, order, and good testimony. The general practices of baptism and the Lord's Supper remain certain, as does the process of church discipline. But the New Testament appears to allow individual churches considerable diversity and freedom in organizing and carrying out their functions. Kevin Cragg and Paul Spikard summarize nicely the loosely bound variety of local church structures:

> As Christians emerged from widely divergent geographic areas, they experimented with various methods of organization. If Jesus had laid down a particular pattern for church government, these early Christians apparently did not know about it. They made ad hoc church government decisions to fit local traditions and personalities. Thus, supporters of virtually any modern form of church government can legitimately claim precedents for their system in the New Testament church experience. A hierarchy of bishops clearly dominated in some locales, especially where leaders had known Jesus before his departure. In other places, a group of elders or presbyters exercised a collective leadership resembling the ordinary synagogue pattern. In still other places, grassroots leadership appeared through efforts to build consensus among the congregation.[2]

---

1. Tacitus, *Annals,* 15.44.
2. In Paul R. Spikard and Kevin M. Cragg, *God's People: A Social History of Christians* (Grand Rapids: Baker, 1994), 35, 37. For a more thorough discussion, see Wayne A. Meeks, *The First Urban Christians: The Social World of the Apostle Paul* (New Haven, Conn.: Yale University Press, 1983), 74–139.

Though considerable diversity is evident among New Testament local churches, congregations were never considered autonomous in the sense of "doing their own thing." Early local churches were always related to the greater community of faith, particularly under apostolic shepherding. Both local leadership and broader apostolic direction are evident, together with the visiting ministries of itinerate teachers and missionaries such as Apollos, Timothy, and Titus.

The Church Related to Israel

After the church's separation from Judaism—most decisively in the A.D. 60s–70s with the destruction of Jerusalem—the post-apostolic writers' perspective regarding the place of ethnic Israel is ambiguous and often skeptical. Influenced in part by Platonic philosophy, Origen (185–254) declared that the truth of the Old Testament was hidden until Jesus Christ. Indeed, he proposed, the Jews had misunderstood their own Scriptures because they interpreted them "according to the mere letter," "in the lowly and contemptible literal phrase."[3] In Origen's view, the Bible is best interpreted *spiritually*. All that is said of Israel must be applied allegorically to the Christian church.[4]

Origen's way of interpreting Scripture was something of a novelty for Christendom in the third century, and most church leaders rejected his neo-platonic reinterpretation of the text. With the passage of time, however, owing to the Jewish dispersion from Palestine and Judaism's rejection of Jesus, it became increasingly difficult to attribute any value to unbelieving Israel in a now Christian era.

Christians were sporadically persecuted for nearly three centuries until Emperor Constantine's supposed conversion and military victories (312–315) led to Christianity becoming the favored religion of the Roman Empire. Increasingly, the church was united with the state. Already, in 321, in the midst of a largely non-Christian empire, Constantine commanded that

---

3. Origen, *On First Principles: Book Four* (Philocalia), 1.2.2; 1.1.7; "taken literally, it [the Old Testament Scripture] is sometimes not only untrue but even unreasonable and impossible" (1.3:4). Origen argues for three levels of interpretation akin to body, soul, and spirit, the latter being the superior.
4. Ibid., 1.3.6.

Sunday be a day of rest so that Christians might appropriately worship. In 325, the emperor himself sponsored and presided over the first ecumenical (all-church) council that debated and then articulated the great Trinitarian declaration known as the Nicene Creed. As more time passed, the empire's taxes financed massive cathedrals and Christian monuments. When the marauding Goths invaded the city of Rome in the early fifth century, the brilliant Augustine (354–430) sought to encourage the Latin Church by writing *The City of God*. Here the famous saint adopted Origen's allegorical method of interpreting the Old Testament: proposing the Christian church as the New Israel and Rome as the New Jerusalem. As the centuries passed, parallels between Old Testament Israel and the Christianized Roman Empire were drawn toward logical conclusions. When Emperor Justinian I (483–565) completed the magnificent Hagia Sophia Cathedral in Constantinople, he is said to have boasted, "Ah-ha, Solomon! Now I have outdone you!" He presumed that his Christian cathedral was superior to the Solomonic temple of Judaism built 1,400 years earlier.

Through Pope Gregory the Great (540–604) and a host of others, the Christian religion became increasingly centralized in a physical, hierarchical, geographical, military, and priestly kingdom. Whereas "tithing" (giving ten percent) was not a common practice in the early church, by the eighth and ninth centuries, an ecclesiastical tithe was instituted as state law in various parts of the by-then *Holy* Roman Empire. Worship on "the Lord's day" was a custom but generally not a commandment in the Old Testament sense of Sabbath law (although some drew the cord tightly).[5] Thomas Aquinas (1225–1274) tried to distinguish between the

---

5. Early church documents such as the *Syriac Didascalia* (c. 250) and *On the Sabbath and Circumcision* (found among the works of Athanasius, d. 373) argue that Sunday was superior to the Sabbath—not a substitute for it—as the day of resurrection and new creation. The *Constitutions of the Holy Apostles* (ca. 380) exhorts Christians to "keep the Sabbath and the Lord's day festival" (7.23). Augustine (d. 430) did not accept literal observance of the fourth commandment and interpreted Sabbath mystically and futuristically. See Samuele Bacchiocchi, "Remembering the Sabbath," in *The Sabbath in Jewish and Christian Traditions*, ed. T. C. Eskenazi, D. J. Harrington, and W. H. Shea (New York: Crossroad, 1991), 78–79; also, Craig Blomberg, "The Sabbath as Fulfilled in Christ," in *The Sabbath in Jewish and Christian Traditions*, 122–28; and D. A. Carson, ed., *From Sabbath to Lord's Day: A Biblical, Historical, and Theological Investigation* (Grand Rapids: Zondervan, 1982).

moral and the ceremonial aspects of the fourth commandment, the former based in natural law (Gen. 2:2–3), which justified the church's imposition of "an elaborate legalistic system of Sunday keeping akin to that of the rabbinical Sabbath."[6] What belonged to Israel in the Old Testament was increasingly assumed by the institutional church: temples, altars, tithes, sacrifices (the mass), the Sabbath, priests, high priest (the pope), special attire, elaborate rituals, and amassing of land and wealth. While sharing a similar ecclesiology with Roman Catholicism, Eastern Orthodoxy (as other families of Orthodoxy) repeatedly suffered invasions and subjugation by Muslims, Mongols, and others, and thus could not enjoy the affluence and development of the Latin West. Yet, as the centuries passed, whether in the East or the West, gone was the New Testament image of the *ekklesia* as a universal, invisible kingdom of priests. No longer was the body of Christ spreading out to make disciples in the uttermost parts of the earth. Even if in the Middle Ages a few courageous missionaries sought to do God's spiritual work as far as China and northern Europe, the Crusades of the eleventh to fourteenth centuries stand as a poignant reminder that confusion of Israel with the church was disastrous. The armies of western Europe were commissioned to war against the Muslims so that in the words of Pope Urban II, "As the times of the Anti-Christ are approaching and as the East, and especially Jerusalem, will be the central point of attack, there must be Christians there to resist."[7] The church had become Israel reincarnate.

A thousand years after Augustine, the Protestant Reformation insisted on turning to the Bible as the sole authority for believers, to salvation by grace through faith alone, and to the priesthood of all believers. These were urgent doctrinal battles to be fought. But in terms of the form and praxis of the church, Protestants and Anglicans largely continued in the footsteps of their Roman Catholic predecessors, except by removing the papacy and the mass. Protestants now constructed their own cathedrals, with their own hierarchy of bishops and their own religious attire. For

---

6. Bacchiocchi, "Remembering the Sabbath," 81; and Aquinas, *Summa Theologica*, 1.2, q.100.3.

7. See John Warwick Montgomery, "Millennium," in *The International Standard Bible Encyclopedia*, ed. G. W. Bromiley, 4 vols. (revised ed., Grand Rapids: Eerdmans, 1986), 4:359.

most, a Christian tithe and Sunday Sabbath remained ecclesiastical mandates, often more rigorously imposed than before. And wars continued to be waged in the name of Christ, more often than not with other "Christian" nations. In truth, the practical structure and functioning of most Protestant churches continued similar to the patterns they had broken away from and, in fact, far more akin to Old Testament Israel than to the New Testament image of the body of Christ.

Evangelical churches, whether in North Atlantic countries or elsewhere in the world, inherited this tradition. We, too, are heirs of an external, centralized vision of what the church should be. For hundreds of millions of Christians, to "serve God" means Sunday attendance at "the house of the Lord" led in a "worship service" by religious professionals who mediate the will of God for the congregation. This is remarkably consistent around the world. Pragmatically, there are advantages to this tradition. It *works,* at least in part. Moreover, it's *safe,* as it perpetuates the forms we have always known. Such thinking about what the church is and how it should function, however, remains indifferent to the teaching of the New Testament.

"Postliberalism" and the Return to Tradition

At this point, some readers may wish to jump ahead to the next chapter for a discussion of the local church. For others, I offer a somewhat more technical but brief discussion about the revival of traditionalism and the accompanying return to a more liturgical, if not High Church, ecclesiology.

With the avalanche of postmodern thinking in the West, some Christians urge a return to formal liturgy and historical Christian traditions. One can surely empathize. In what can seem like a world gone mad, a reaffirmed continuity with historical Christian faith is a welcome call. Who has not, in the midst of city noise, found a haven of sanity and refreshment in the silence and beauty of a cathedral? In the sometimes strange worlds of Christian television and evangelical entertainment, where certain biblical doctrines might be set aside in favor of emotive preaching or a good tune, the High Church with its dignity, intelligence, and theological moorings may provide wonderful relief. So it is not surprising that some today are fleeing evangelical and Pentecostal churches for the hallowed ritual, historical continuity, and quiet awe of the cathedral—whether Protestant, Anglican, Roman Catholic, or Eastern Orthodox. And for renewal within mainline denominations, we must thank God.

While sincere believers desire to reexperience the sacredness of God in this return to the High Church, other factors provide a more general attraction to Christian tradition. One significant motivation for such a shift is *postliberal* theology. In North American divinity schools today, postliberal theology denotes a movement that rejects liberal skepticism regarding the Bible in favor of an emphasis on biblical *narrative* (the *stories* of the Bible).[8] In some ways, the movement steps away from theological liberalism's disbelief in much of Christian teaching, with the intention of reaffirming the Bible as the basis for Christian faith. However, in postmodern theology, Scripture is not understood as the infallible Word of God as in classical Christian faith; rather, the Bible—especially the New Testament—serves as the *expression* of faith (or testimony) in the earliest Christian community. Centered in the Synoptic Gospels' *story* of Jesus, living Christian faith is perceived as being passed down through tradition–history in the ongoing life of the believing community. In other words, the *way* in which the early church responded to God's working in Jesus Christ should continue to characterize the way believers today respond to Jesus and to God (albeit often within very different Christian traditions).

Postliberalism argues that Christian doctrines are not to be understood as ultimate (or universal) truths, but instead serve as *rules* or *communally authoritative teachings* that organize life within a particular

---

8. The term *postliberalism* is usually associated with Yale theologian George A. Lindbeck, although the movement draws on both the narrative approach to Scripture by Hans Frei and the philosophy of Alasdair MacIntyre. Having coalesced rather loosely as a movement in the 1980s, today exponents include Stanley Hauerwas, William Placher, and Kathyrn Tanner. Evangelical theologians in dialogue with postliberalism include Alister McGrath and Stanley Grenz. See G. Lindbeck, *The Nature of Doctrine: Religion and Theology in a Postliberal Age* (Philadelphia: Westminster, 1984); Lindbeck, *The Church in a Postliberal Age* (Grand Rapids: Eerdmans, 2003); also Daniel Liechty, *Reflecting on Faith in a Post-Christian Time* (Telford, Penn.: Cascadia; Scottdale, Penn.: Herald Press, 2003).

believing tradition. In a post-Kantian or postmodern framework, *truth* can no longer be spoken of in a universal sense. It is always interpretive. Truth is seen as intra-systemic, formed by a web of influences around us, rather than having a separate reality. Therefore, because all thought and experience are culturally and linguistically defined, postliberalism argues that the point of religious faith is neither adhering to certain doctrines (as in classical Christianity and evangelicalism) nor elevating individual experience (as in modern liberalism). Instead, the religious life should focus on interiorizing and living out the understanding of reality within a particular believing community. In postliberalism, Christian faith is necessarily tied to its expression within a particular church tradition and community. Christian tradition becomes the expression and guardian of believing faith. Hence, for theological reasons, some people today are returning to the older Christian traditions and High Church formality, having concluded that not much else can be trusted.

From a biblical perspective, however, truth is not simply interpretive. Rather, truth is grounded in the self-revelation of the triune God. Though we will never grasp all truth in an exhaustive sense, there is real truth to be apprehended because God has spoken. He has objectively come to us in the incarnation of the Son and in the words of the Bible. Just because our understanding of truth is conditioned by our finitude and fallenness does not mean "true truth" does not exist or is unknowable. In the words of theologian Alister McGrath, "Scripture has authority not because of what the Christian community has chosen to make of it, but because of what it *is*, and what it conveys."[9] If postliberalism's return to tradition serves as merely a Christianized haven in a world of relativism, then it falls well short of the biblical truth foundational to vital Christian faith.

All of this brings us to the main point of our discussion. Some have moved toward the liturgical High Church for motives that are surely laudable. Evangelicals continue to grow in number in several mainline traditions. Moreover, the New Testament permits considerable diversity for local church forms and cultural expression. Nevertheless, it is unlikely

---

9. Alister E. McGrath, *A Passion for Truth: The Intellectual Coherence of Evangelicalism* (Downers Grove, Ill.: InterVarsity, 1996), 155–56, see 119–200; see also Timothy R. Phillips and Dennis Okholm, eds., *The Nature of Confession: Evangelicals and Postliberals in Conversation* (Downers Grove, Ill.: InterVarsity, 1996).

that New Testament teaching about the nature of the church has in itself been the motivation for the return to tradition. The code for reexperiencing the purpose of the church is not found by retreating into liturgy and cathedrals but by understanding and applying afresh New Testament principles for the church. The blueprint for a dynamic Christian community is the Word of God. While cultural, traditional, and denominational interpretations of the church are to be appreciated, all forms of Christ's church must be finally subject to Scripture, lest in their drift they increasingly cease to be Christian at all.

Conclusion

We have seen that in the New Testament the body of Christ is primarily a spiritual entity, a living organism under the headship of the Savior and guided by the Spirit to the glory of the Father. Diametrically different from the centralized kingdom of God in Israel, the universal church can be characterized as decentralized—that is, no longer focused in a particular race, geography, Sabbath, or hierarchy of priests. Although the earliest churches manifested this spiritual reality and freedom, the recentralization of the church through Rome's political power reversed much of what the New Testament seemed to promise. Unfortunately, neither the Reformation nor numerous subsequent movements succeeded in restoring the *ekklesia* that was largely lost.

We have seen also that in recent decades, some have again turned to traditional and High Church ecclesiologies. One factor in this return is postliberalism's emphasis that the gospel testimony about Jesus is carried down through history in the believing traditions. We are reminded of the importance of the community as formative for Christian life and as the context in which belief is worked out in practice. However, postliberalism builds on the postmodern premise that truth and doctrine can *only* be understood as communitarian perceptions; true truth is cognitively unknowable. Rather than the Bible, the community itself, with its traditions of belief and practice, becomes the generator of true Christian faith today. Some therefore turn to traditional ecclesiologies in hopes that there they will experience the vital Christian life reminiscent of that in the New Testament. I have suggested that we do well to return to the biblical fount itself, not only for an example of dynamic belief, but also as instructive of God's design for the body of Christ and its expression in today's local churches.

All of this has been rather complicated. We return to our practical theme of what the church should be. What are the New Testament foundations for the church? What does a biblical theology of the universal church (seen in these last chapters) imply for our own congregations? Is not the New Testament addressed primarily to specific *local churches*? If so, doesn't the Bible set forth guidelines as to how the local church should function? We will turn now to explore the local church as the *finite form* of the body of Christ in the world.

Chapter 5

WHAT IS THE LOCAL CHURCH?

Over pizza one night, a senior denominational missionary complained, "Those who push the idea of the universal church usually do not have a theology of the local church." Referring to parachurch organizations, he was concerned that for many believers such organizations substitute for the local church. Such suspicions have merit. Yet his vision of the *ekklesia* may be too small.

In emphasizing the universal church as the central concept through which we interpret the local congregation, the importance of the local church is fortified, not diminished. Though the local church is not an absolute in itself or an exclusive means of serving God, it exists as the tangible form for fulfilling the purposes of the body of Christ in the world. It is important to define the local church and its fundamental purposes vis-à-vis the New Testament. Having explored the distinctions between the body of Christ and Israel in previous chapters, we now unfold more fully the relationship between the universal church and the local church.

A Practical Definition

If you are like most people, you will define the local church in glowing ideals. The high hopes we have for our congregations may explain why discouragement can so easily overtake those who labor long hours in local churches. Our ideals differ from our actual experience. In the early church, as today, congregations often fell short of what even their own members wished they would be. Often, those who sing their church's praises are not close to the weekly crises and conflicts that are part of a local church's functioning in a fallen world.

Of course, we need high goals for our congregations (and the next chapters will address them more adequately). For now, we will employ a simple, realistic definition that I believe corresponds with the ecclesial portraits of the New Testament. That is, we should conceive of the local church as it *is*, rather than as it *ought* to be. Therefore, we can say that the local church is composed of *professing believers in Jesus Christ who have been baptized, practice the Lord's Supper, and organize to do God's will.*[1] Such a definition includes churches at Corinth, Galatia, Sardis, and Laodicea that were far from ideal (as were many of the assemblies in the New Testament). The above definition implies seven basic aspects of the local assembly.

Seven Basic Aspects of the Local Church

Professing Believers in Jesus Christ

The local church is composed of people who *call* themselves *Christians.* If a person does not confess faith in Jesus as Lord, he or she may attend services but is almost never included in membership. Throughout Christian history, virtually all churches require the profession that Jesus Christ is the Son of God. Nevertheless, from God's perspective, the parable about the wheat and the tares (Matt. 13:24–30) implies that the local church can include those who have never been born-again—despite their profession. This is especially true in contexts of cultural Christianity—for example, in state churches, in families who for generations have attended church, or in tribal conversions decided by a chief or council. In seventeenth-century New England, Puritan churches baptized infants

---

1. I have appropriated and modified the definition from Charles C. Ryrie, *A Survey of Bible Doctrine* (Chicago: Moody, 1972), 141–42.

for church membership, but some of those infants grew up to be voting members who no longer believed in certain historical doctrines. A well-known popularizer of the "God is dead" movement recently testified that on the night before his ordination into a historic Christian denomination he had an "epiphany of Satan," a powerful experience that impelled his trajectory into what can only be described as atheism. Even in traditions where those seeking membership are rigorously examined, there are no guarantees that all members have placed saving faith in Christ. The long-time pastor of one of the largest Baptist churches in North America once declared—no doubt on a bad day—that as much as seventy-five percent of his membership may not be "born again." Certainly most local churches, whatever the testimonies and catechisms required, include both regenerate and unregenerate individuals.

Doctrine

Those who confess faith in Christ adhere to at least a minimal theology regarding the Savior. They declare that Jesus is "the Lord" and "the Son of God," however broadly theological modernism might define such titles. All orthodox Christians declare that Jesus Christ is the eternally "begotten Son," the incarnate "one and only Son" of God the Father, within the three persons of the Holy Trinity. We declare that the Word fully assumed human nature and was born of the Virgin Mary. We profess that Jesus lived a perfect life, revealing both the essence of God and the essence of man as divinely intended. Christ died as our Substitute and Redeemer at the Cross, was resurrected from the dead, ascended into heaven, and is glorified at the right hand of God the Father. He will return again to judge human-kind. Whether the Apostles' Creed or any other doctrinal statement, a pro-fession of faith involves at least an elementary level of theology. With very few exceptions, a local church will subscribe to a particular confession, creed, or theological statement. Doctrinal content is essential for the church to continue in the apostles' teaching (Acts 2:42), "the faith that was once for all entrusted to the saints" (Jude 3). In the New Testament, the teaching of sound doctrine is commanded (1 Tim. 4:16; Titus 1:9; 2:1), and false doctrine sternly warned against (1 Tim. 4:1–11; 2 Peter 2:1–22).

Doctrine also presumes a basis of authority. Whether Eastern

Orthodox, Roman Catholic, Protestant, Evangelical, or Pentecostal, all classical theology declares the Holy Scripture as inspired, authoritative, and infallible. All have affirmed as official canon at least the thirty-nine books of the Jewish Old Testament, already largely in place by the time of Jesus and probably much earlier; this corresponds with the decision of Judaism's Council of Jamnia in A.D. 90. As for the New Testament, whereas *official* recognition of the Christian canon occurred only at the Councils of Hippo (A.D. 393) and Carthage (A.D. 397), virtually all twenty-seven books circulated as Scripture by A.D. 200, and lists of authoritative books were recognized as early as A.D. 125. The New Testament itself claims equal status with the Old Testament as Scripture (Heb. 1:1–3; 2 Peter 3:15–16; Rev. 22:16–19). Jesus often refers to the Hebrew Scriptures as the final, binding authority in theological disputes (Matt. 22:29–32, 43–45; John 10:35), yet those Scriptures were both fulfilled and superseded by his own word and that which would be given by the Spirit to his disciples (Matt. 24:35; John 16:13). Thus, the early church simply followed the Lord's directive in upholding Scripture as the final arbiter of truth. Regarding the preeminence of the Bible in the first three centuries of the church, Hans von Campenhausen concludes, "So holy Scripture remains without qualification the supreme authority, and the one fixed norm of teaching and morals for the orthodox church."[2] We conclude that to confess Jesus Christ as the "Lord" and "Son of God" already invokes some expression of doctrine, and all historical Christian communities ground that theological content, above all else, in the Bible.

Water Baptism

Jesus Christ commissioned baptism. Regardless of the initiate's age or the preferred method of water baptism, churches throughout the history of Christendom have required baptism for membership. The pattern is established in the New Testament, where new believers were immediately baptized in water when they were accepted into the church. Nor do any exceptions to this practice appear in the Christian Scriptures.

---

2. Hans von Campenhausen, *The Formation of the Christian Bible*, trans. J. A. Baker (Philadelphia: Fortress, 1972), 329.

In contrast to the repeated washings for purification in Judaism and pagan Hellenism, Christian baptism is a once-for-all act. Similar to Jewish ritual baptism, the early church practiced water baptism by immersion until at least the fifth century, with infrequent instances of pouring as a substitute—although the practice of *aspersion* (pouring) is evident as early as about A.D. 120 in the *Didache*. Around A.D. 200, Hippolytus and Tertullian separately describe baptismal ceremonies for candidates who completed three years of required catechism.³ On the day of baptism (often Easter), the Holy Spirit was petitioned to come upon the baptismal waters, the candidate disrobed, renounced Satan and all his works, and was anointed with oil to banish all evil spirits. Standing in the water, the candidate confessed faith in each person of the Trinity and was immersed three times, once after each confession. He was then anointed, reclothed, and received the laying on of hands, symbolizing the reception of the Spirit. The members of the congregation then gave the kiss of peace and proceeded to the Lord's Supper, when for the first time the newly baptized were allowed to participate in the Eucharist and prayer. Whereas the earliest reference to infant baptism is found in Tertullian's *On Baptism* (ca. A.D. 200), the baptism of believers was clearly normative in the early centuries of the church. During the fourth and fifth centuries, virtually every leader of the Eastern and Western churches, even those born to Christian parents—such as Chrysostom, Jerome, and the Cappadocian Fathers—were baptized as believing adults.⁴ Thus, water baptism was considered the initiatory rite, as we have seen, for one to enter the community of faith. This does not prohibit baptism for those like the Ethiopian eunuch who are without a specific congregation (Matt. 28:19; Acts 8:38–39). But it does indicate that no Christian congregation is formed without baptized members. That is, throughout the history of Christendom, with very rare exceptions, local churches do not admit as members anyone who has not by some mode been baptized in water.

3. Hippolytus, *Apostolic Tradition;* Tertullian, *On Baptism;* an even earlier source is Justin Martyr, *First Apology,* 61, 65.
4. Everett Ferguson, "baptism," in *Encyclopedia of Early Christianity,* ed. E. Ferguson (New York: Garland, 1990), 131–34; Geoffrey Wainwright, "baptism," in *The Encyclopedia of Christianity,* ed. Erwin Fahlbusch et al. (Grand Rapids: Eerdmans; Leiden: Brill, 1999), 2.184–88.

The Lord's Supper

Once-for-all baptism initiates a believer into the practice of the Lord's Supper, instituted by Jesus Christ as the foremost practice of Christian worship (Matt. 26:26–29; Luke 22:14–20; 1 Cor. 11:23–26). Similar to baptism, the Eucharist directly symbolizes the death of the Lord Jesus for the sin of the world. The Communion formula recalls the Lord's resurrection and his coming again. Participation includes individual and communitarian confession and mutual forgiveness of sin, just as we have been forgiven. Although most parachurch organizations, similar to local churches, are composed of baptized believers who purpose to do God's will, it has traditionally been the prerogative of the local church to gather around the Lord's Supper. Indeed, almost all Christian communities have restricted the Eucharist to the church, even though no New Testament commandment does so.

Different terms describe this act: "breaking bread" (Acts 2:46; 20:7, 11; 1 Cor. 10:16); "the Lord's Supper" (1 Cor. 11:20); and "gather[ing] together" or *synaxis* (as in the non-canonical 1 Clement 34:7). In the early second century, the term for the opening prayer of "thanksgiving" (Greek *eucharistia,* see 1 Cor. 11:24) became the common term for the entire event, that is, the Eucharist. Around the same period, the partaking of the bread and the wine was separated as ritual from a larger communal meal shared by the entire congregation (1 Cor. 10:16). The Eucharist is the new Passover meal for the Christian. The Savior's death is the means for redemption from sin and the unification as a new people under the headship of the new Moses and deliverer. Thus, symbolized in the Lord's Supper, the Cross became the basis for fellowship through the payment by Christ's blood for sin and through the Holy Spirit's indwelling that yokes the believer with the Head and with the members of the body of Christ.

Therefore, biblically and historically, a local church is characterized by both baptism and the Lord's Supper. Although these practices are not necessarily illicit when practiced outside a specific local church (Acts 2:46), they unite and help define the local church. As we remember the emphasis also on sound doctrine, the judgment of John Calvin is instructive: "Whenever we see the Word of God purely preached and listened to, and the sacraments administered according to Christ's institution, it is in no way to be doubted that a church of God exists."[5]

Implies Membership

Any social entity demands commitment, be it through official or merely functional membership. Today's church membership rolls often appear to be more a pragmatic formality than a biblically based reality. Nevertheless, New Testament churches did evince sufficient organization to determine various levels of leadership, to send letters of recommendation on behalf of good-standing members as they traveled, and to discipline and even excommunicate members who fell into sin. In Western culture, church membership may be likened to the step from dating to engagement and marriage. It signifies commitment to a specific congregation. Ideally, church membership establishes one's spiritual family and helps strengthen mutual accountability. A local church without some form of membership leaves participants no organized way to correct errant or even cult-like leadership. Conversely, virtuous leaders lack appropriate structures to correct rebellious participants. In the New Testament, possibly excepting one's physical family, the local church constitutes the circle of relationships to which believers are most closely identified and to which they are held responsible by the Lord himself.

Organization

Following our definition of the local church, if every congregation is purposed "to do God's will," then all churches, from the most anti-institutional to the most hierarchical, will have organization. An organization might be constructive or it might be disastrous. But it is impossible to function in community without patterns and structure.

Two extremes are to be avoided. At one pole are churches that despise the idea of formal organization. A few have claimed, "We only want to follow the Spirit." One such group in the late 1960s was a community

---

5. John Calvin, *Institutes of the Christian Religion*, 4.1.9, see also 1.10.

in Goleta, California, composed of several well-known leaders coming out of superchurches and large bureaucratic organizations. But, though the Spirit may move, it's hard for mortals to find the groove. For lack of coordination, such groups rarely survive beyond a few months or years. In the twenty-first century, we are seeing a proliferation of innovative forms, whether Holy Spirit communities or postmodern experiments. Thousands of these groups will likely dissolve for simple lack of structure.

If one pole represents resistance to organization, other churches are so excessively regimented, so obsessively structured, that they disallow the Christian community to be a living organism. Little if any place exists for spontaneity or freedom in the Holy Spirit. Clearly, larger numbers of people require increased organization. God gives the gift of administration to the church. Good administration establishes a structure in which the other gifts of the Spirit are maximized. Talents and abilities are harmonized and set free in the service of our Lord. Nevertheless, in some churches, regardless of size, the organization becomes repressive. Whether it's a megachurch ministering to thousands or a rural parish chapel, a local church can become so locked into organization that it suffocates rather than breathes the presence of God. Such churches de-characterize the personal Lord of the church—our actively triune God, the One-and-Three, who is community. Organization is necessary, but it is not an end in itself. It must be flexibly at the disposal of the Head of the church, Jesus Christ, through the actuation of the Holy Spirit.

Indeed, the local church is to reflect the tripersonal reality of the God of the Bible. The New Testament descriptions of the relationships between the Father, the Son, and the Holy Spirit describe both equality of nature yet functional order. The Father loves the Son and gives to him all honor, all glory, all judgment, and all things. Yet the Son does not hoard such astounding benefits; rather, at the end of time, he lays "everything" back at the feet of the Father (1 Cor. 15:24-28). Nor does the Spirit glorify himself; rather, his delight is to glorify the Son (John 16:14). In the Holy Trinity we see reciprocity and generosity, each to the other, while each divine person fulfills his place in God's working (or economy) in creation. The perfect model for the church, as *imago ecclesiasticus*, is the Christian Godhead itself. Therefore, however it might be culturally expressed, the very organization of the local church should be characterized by the equality and order revealed in God's very being.

In my opinion, as implied in the previous chapter, there is an ecclesiological evolution from the infant congregation of Pentecost to the bishopric of the seven churches in the book of Revelation (chapters 2–3). Though the details may be argued, at the core is the fact that there is not *one* ecclesiastical structure in the New Testament but a *plurality* of models. Of note is that the Koine Greek of Paul's time had dozens of words related to organization. Nevertheless, although the apostle calls for *order (taxis)* in the local church (1 Cor. 14:40; Col. 2:5), he exercises considerable restraint in prescribing how this order should be maintained in each assembly.[6] Though certain rules of order appear clear and universal, such as instructions regarding the Lord's Supper, the qualifications of leadership, and the discipline of errant members, Paul and the other New Testament writers are rarely *prescriptive* regarding the organization and forms of the local church. Paul's instructions to the churches "involved granting them a considerable degree of autonomy."[7] Indeed, the primary metaphors for the life of the congregation are highly personalistic in nature—God is "Father," and believers are "children," "brothers," and "sisters." Paul calls himself a "father" (1 Cor. 4:14–15; 2 Cor. 12:14; 1 Thess. 2:11) and a "mother" who suffers labor pains (Gal. 4:19), urging others "to grow up" and become adults in the faith (1 Cor. 3:10–15). The local church is to understand itself as part of the bride of Christ, the body of Christ, and the household of faith. Organization was present but not primary.

Although one particular structure or another might be closer to the general ideal of the church as portrayed in the New Testament, this

---

6. Robert J. Banks, "Church Order and Government," in *Dictionary of Paul and His Letters*, ed. G. F. Hawthorne, R. P. Martin, and D. G. Reid (Downers Grove, Ill.: InterVarsity, 1993), 132. "Unlike the Greeks, he does not use the word *taxis* of an office that is responsible for ensuring that order is maintained. . . . This is everyone's responsibility as they share what the Spirit grants them (1 Cor. 12:7–11) and discern what the Spirit is contributing through others (1 Cor. 14:28, 30, 32). The church's 'liturgy' is a communal construction. Order stems from a highly participatory and charismatic process and is not determined in advance by a few. Though neither purely spontaneous nor fully egalitarian, it is dynamic and mutually created."

7. Ibid., 133.

ecclesiological plurality is nonetheless instructive and liberating. Latitude in ecclesial forms in the first century frees us to create and experiment with diverse models of the church today. For example, certain cultures—notably in Africa and Latin America—seem to prefer strong singular leadership and direction from the center. Others cultures, such as Japan and the North Atlantic countries, often respond best to plurality of leadership or even democratic governance. Although multiple elder leadership perhaps best approaches the ideal for the local church, every structure of leadership involves weaknesses as well as strengths.[8] Within the parameters of the New Testament, different mixes of peoples and subcultures may develop forms that maximize their calling from God. The real absolute of the local church is not the outer shell, the organization, or the patterns of ritual; rather, our ecclesiological forms exist to serve something far greater.

The Local Church Exists to Do God's Will

The local church is composed of *professing believers in Jesus Christ who have been baptized, practice the Lord's Supper, and organize to do God's will.* That is, aspects that define a Christian congregation include: people who confess faith in Jesus Christ; doctrine (as beliefs and parameters) ultimately based on the Bible; water baptism; regular participation in the Lord's Supper; membership, whether formal or informal; organization; and intention to do God's will. The last phrase of our definition, "to do God's will," is the heart of what a biblical ecclesiology is all about. But what is God's will for a local church? Virtually all local churches articulate goals—often very good goals. The moorings securing these goals, however, are not always well founded in the New Testament. Even when biblical objectives are articulated, the weekly energy of the church is often spent in activities quite peripheral to the body's main purpose. In short, the forms, structures, and methods we use must be defined by the answer to this question: What is God's will for a local church?

---

8. See Gene A. Getz, *Elders and Leaders: God's Plan for Leading the Church: A Biblical, Historical, and Cultural Perspective* (Chicago: Moody, 2003).

Chapter 6

WHAT WE DO REVEALS WHO WE ARE

FUNCTIONING AS CHURCH

Theological treatments of the local church often begin with a survey concerning various ecclesiastical structures. The local church is interpreted in terms of a theological tradition or a denominational system. For example, a church is classified by its form of government, whether congregational, representative, or episcopal—that is, by bottom-up, reciprocal, or top-down management structures. As such, a group of Christians is given identity by its organization.

The Bible, however, does not do this. At the beginning of the church in Acts 2:42–47, the New Testament centers its description of the local church particularly in its *activities,* a pattern reiterated all the way through to Christ's admonitions to the seven churches of Revelation. What a New Testament church *is,* or is *supposed* to be, can best be identified by what it *does* in fulfilling the will of God. That is, the local church is especially distinguished by its response to the Head of the body—even, as we earlier observed, in the obedience of baptism and the Lord's Supper. The actions in Acts 2 characterize a people indwelled by the Holy Spirit, the Spirit of Christ. Instead of buildings, Christian Sabbaths, programs, and clergy, the *vital functions* of the early church help identify "the will of God" that our congregations today should accomplish. In surveying the New Testament from Pentecost to the end of Revelation, one discerns four basic categories of activities that mark the local church: *worship, learning, fellowship,* and *evangelism/mission.* Virtually all the activities and energy of the early church divide across these four areas.[1] Because specific actions of the early church sometimes can reflect situations and cultures different from our own, we will focus on the broader principles or *functions* of New Testament activities.[2] These living functions define the *why,* the center, the practical essence of the local church.

Worship

From the beginning, the church was characterized by honoring the Lord God and his Son Jesus Christ. The believers "devoted themselves . . . to prayer" (Acts 2:42); "everyone was filled with awe" (v. 43); "they broke bread in their homes" (v. 46), "praising God" (v. 47). The early church seemed to recognize that it existed preeminently for the glory of God. Adoration and praise spilled over into everything. Amazement, wonder, and the fear of the Lord characterized the church before the holy, gracious Father and his resurrected Son Jesus Christ. With the indwelling of the Holy Spirit, believers perceived themselves as the living temple of God's presence. From the very beginning, the Lord's Supper became a focal point of worship activity. Participation in the Eucharist—the breaking of bread and the drinking from the cup—served as the highest expression of sacred worship. Indeed, it is the Christian's Holy of Holies (1 Cor. 11:23–33). In the first century, collective worship included singing, reading of Scriptures (especially Psalms), sacrifice of one's material possessions (gifts, offerings), and prayers of adoration to God and Christ.[3] Worship characterized not only official assemblies of believers but also spontaneous occasions when a few believers simply, if not randomly, met together.

---

1. See the appendix, "Four Functions or More?" for a discussion of other activities not considered as functional paradigms of the local church.
2. Aubrey Malphurs, *Doing Church: A Biblical Guide for Leading Ministries Through Change* (Grand Rapids: Kregel, 1999), 89–111. Malphurs is very helpful in discussing the need to discern between New Testament patterns versus principles, as well as between New Testament forms and functions.
3. See Acts 4:23–31; 13:2–3; Ephesians 5:18–20; 6:18; Colossians 3:16.

As the new bride of Christ, the earliest church effervesces with creative love. To be creative means to be *innovative* and at the same time *authentic* to who we are as individuals and who we are as believing communities. Lamentably, some churches today close themselves off from innovation and authenticity because of questions about styles of music or the legitimacy of applause or expressions of praise. Interestingly, the fifth-century expositor John Chrysostom, bothered by applause during his messages, declared that he did not think the response fitting—to which the people applauded all the more! It seems his listeners were agreeing with the "golden-mouthed" orator, but they did not know how else to express themselves. Tensions often flare around the imitating of one form of worship or the avoidance of another. Rather than our "cloistering in" to avoid worship styles that make us uncomfortable, we should think creatively about fresh forms of worship that express ourselves authentically to the Lord. Though some forms of worship have more of a biblical basis than others, God has given us freedom to invent new forms of worship—forms that spring forth from the depths of who we are within our own congregation and within our own cultural setting.

In Brazil, for example, the Aliança Bíblica/World Team churches enjoy a form of the Lord's Supper that is profoundly transformative. A large table is prepared with various sets of bread and cups of wine, each accompanied by two or three chairs. Arrayed around the Lord's Table is a wider circle, with as many chairs as participants. As members sit in the large circle around the table, they begin the observance by singing worship songs, which soon merge with the quiet prayers of individuals or small clusters of worshipers. As the Spirit of God moves in their midst, one member might cross the circle to pray with someone else, while others continue to pray alone or continue in song. Sins are confessed. Worship and intercession grow. Groups of two or three spontaneously advance to the chairs at the Lord's Table. As they continue in prayer, now at the Table, it is not uncommon for members to ask forgiveness of one another—church leaders and deacons, women at odds with one another, husbands and wives—as each prepares to partake of the bread. With multiple sets of elements available, there is room for several groups to sit at the Table and partake of the Lord's Supper. Some two- or threesomes may choose to remain in prayer at the Table for a time prior to offering the elements to one another. After they break the bread and drink the cup, these leave the Lord's Table as others take their place. Occasionally, a person will partake more than once with different members of the circle as the deepest form of both worship and fellowship combined. All the while, small groups continue to pray quietly in the wider circle. This practice of the Lord's Supper often continues for two hours or more. As believers seek deep cleansing before God and transparent reconciliation with one another through this special practice of the Lord's Supper, the collective spirit of the church is recentered and given new life in Christ. Of course, whether this particular form of worship would help your church is not the point. Rather, each local church has opportunity, through the power of the Holy Spirit, to develop fresh ways to glorify God.

Too often, our expectation of a "worship program" amounts to little more than a moving prayer and nice music. Many of us have little experience in communal worship where the presence of the Lord is both openly sought and emotionally experienced. No doubt some folks seek emotional gratification rather than true rendering of honor to the Father, the Son and the Holy Spirit. Yet many people yearn to *participate* in giving honor to God, using all of their senses—smelling, touching, seeing, tasting, *and* hearing—as seen in more collective worship styles among Latin and African-American congregations. As biblical truth and self-honesty help guide us, the New Testament provides us with freedom to experiment and to innovate with original expressions of worship whereby the local church might enter more fully into the delight of the Lord. Though teaching, fellowship, and evangelism also are vital activities, nothing is more central to the local assembly than worship. Worship is the privileged calling and occupation of every believer in every local church. And this activity will continue for all eternity.

Learning

"They devoted themselves to the apostles' teaching" (Acts 2:42). In light of an increasing negativism toward "theology" among millions of evangelicals around the world, it is surprising how frequently the Bible speaks of teaching, doctrine, and example. Jesus is called *teacher* (Gk. *didaskalos;* Heb. *rabbi*) about forty times in the New Testament (of only fifty-eight times total). The verb *to teach (didasko)* and the noun *teaching* or *doctrine (didache)* are repeated another 127 times in the New Testament—usually with positive connotations. Teachers such as Apollos (Acts 18:24–28) stand in high esteem in the early church. In the short pastoral letters of 1 and 2 Timothy and Titus alone, we find nearly fifty references to instruction, doctrine, and teaching by example—all with a view to believers maturing in consecration before the Lord. Paul charges Timothy, "Watch your life and your doctrine closely. Persevere in them, because if you do, you will save both yourself and your hearers" (1 Tim. 4:16). To Titus he writes, "You must teach what is in accord with sound doctrine" (Titus 2:1). The Bible insists that teaching is foundational to the believer's life (Rom. 12:2; Eph. 4:11–13). Knowing the Word of God opens the door to knowing the God of the Word. In an age in which lax study, subjectivism, and prophetic "visions" rule many pulpits of the world, it is essential that the church diligently teach the biblical doctrines and principles of the faith (Jude 3). A primary function of the local church, then, is to teach correctly about the God of the Bible and develop its members' understanding as to how to live rightly for Christ. Indeed, if believers are not steadily and convincingly learning truths that nurture them in the Lord, then the local church is failing in its God-given responsibility.

Neither the term *teaching* nor its effect as *learning* captures the breadth of the New Testament concept of believers growing in understanding and capacity for godly life. The idea involves far more than the impartation and appropriation of knowledge. Teaching in the wider biblical sense includes various stimuli to faithfulness. One of these is the diversity of testimonies and examples in the local church. Consecrated singles, joyous young families, unashamed professionals, and dedicated missionaries all serve as role models for people in a multiplicity of ways. Examples of living faith invite us to trust God beyond our horizons. Good evidence indicates that the apostle Thomas carried the gospel from Jerusalem to India, preaching and making disciples; yet, equally powerful was his testimony in apparent martyrdom. Since the first century, the Indian church has endured hardships of many kinds, yet it stands in part because of Thomas's obedience to Jesus Christ. Learning is generated both by the power of the Word and by examples of faithfulness.

The massive Pentecostal movement, especially in non-North Atlantic countries, continues to be pushed onward by examples of faith, zeal, and sacrifice. Whereas the theological content of Christian faith is important, the Bible is equally clear that teaching also must occur by contagious testimony. The preaching of the Word without challenging examples of trust and sacrifice often leads to complacency and hardening of hearts.

Jesus' mandate extends beyond "teaching them to obey everything I have commanded you" to also "go and make disciples" (Matt. 28:19–20). We teach and call others to follow. Yet, discipleship does not mean that we as leaders create *our* own disciples, meaning followers of ourselves. It is instructive that the word *disciple* almost disappears from the New Testament not long after Pentecost. Jesus calls us to facilitate others in following *him* so as to hear *his* voice, to love *him,* and obey *him* as Head of the body (Acts 6:7). This implies that pastors loosen their grip on the local church and raise up others to do the ministry as coleaders, if not copastors. In virtually all foreign mission endeavors, the purpose of discipleship is to train qualified nationals to preach, evangelize, baptize, organize, and pastor in the missionary's stead. I have often wondered why so few North American pastors do the same in their own congregations. Commenting on "First World" Christianity, observers from other parts of the world often note that the professionalization of ministry has contributed to an increasingly ingrown and anemic church. One of the great strengths of the mushrooming "Two-Thirds World" church is the communality of ministry as every believer's obligation and joy.

Sunday school has its virtues, and expository preaching as well, but the local church can create alternative forms of communicating the truth and instilling in others a positive Christian faith. Didactic forms of preaching and teaching must continue. Yet, as Jesus exemplified with the disciples, the greatest methodology of all is learning by participation. I have never experienced more intense learning than I did during months of evangelizing door-to-door all day long and preaching in the streets at night in Trinidad and Tobago. Each house seemed to be a different religious mixture of Hinduism, Jehovah's Witness, Anglicanism, and Shango (spiritism). Yet in this syncretistic environment, my friends and I learned to trust the Holy Spirit and to share the gospel with boldness. The most powerful form of learning, as Rabbi Jesus demonstrated with his various levels of discipleship, is firsthand experience through taking steps of faith. In short, the multiform biblical teaching–learning process is what pushes us forward and, in turn, deepens and strengthens the other vital functions that should characterize the church.

Fellowship

Several months ago, a seminary student raised in a communist home in eastern Europe asked with tears why it was so hard to make friends in the United States. Her faith in Christ had led to discrimination on many sides in her native country, yet there she had forged strong bonds with her fellow believers. As often happens when believers come to faith amid repression and hardship, the local church became her family and her lifeline. After coming to North America, she had repeatedly tried to build Christian ties with others, but to little avail. Cultural differences aside, the problem was likely not with her. Despite our freedom of association and religious expression, as a culture we are more socially estranged than at any time in history. Even those renewed in Christ carry the effects of having been raised in day-care facilities or broken homes, with changing dads, moms, or siblings, or moving from school to school and city to city. Multitudes today lack meaningful relationships with anyone. Like orphans who have never experienced human bonding, many people in our urban society—Christians included—have minimal capacity for meaningful friendship.

Recounting the birth of the church at Pentecost, Luke writes, "They devoted themselves . . . to the fellowship" (Acts 2:42). "All the believers were together and had everything in common" (v. 44). "They broke bread in their homes and ate together with glad and sincere hearts" (v. 46). In the everyday language of the ancient world, the Greek word for fellowship, *koinonia*, sometimes described the marital relationship. In the New Testament, the term occurs twenty times, referring both to our personal communion with God, or, more often, to a believer's affinity with other Christians (1 John 1:3, 6–7). Thus, in a biblical sense, *fellowship* does not refer to casual connections around mutual interests such as sports or school. Nor do gatherings around church meals necessarily guarantee biblical fellowship, inasmuch as nearly all people groups enjoy corporate meals of some kind. Instead, Christian *koinonia* signifies the deepest of human relationships through mutual openness and heartfelt commitment around love for our Lord.

A hunger for relationship is intrinsic to our regeneration in Christ, but churches today often experience little Christ-centered fellowship. In urban North America, our mobile and crowded lifestyles make true *koinonia* elusive. On a typical Sunday morning, most Christians sit passively for one to two hours listening to a teacher or preacher—not unlike in a theater. Though we sit in the midst of a crowd, we're largely isolated. Our attendance at a worship service implies a desire to encounter God, but more than a few people have abandoned expectations of having substantial friendships at church.

The commands of the New Testament directly address our relationship with other believers more frequently than our behavior in the world or even our vertical responsibilities with God. Or put another way, a person's true relationship with God is most visible in horizontal relationships with others in the local church. Of course, some will argue that doctrinal truth itself is the most important aspect of the Christian life. However, as important as the defense of Christian truth is, it cannot be disengaged from the New Testament imperative for believers to love and care for one another. The some sixty-four "one another" passages in the New Testament suggest that our relationship to God and real understanding of truth are measured in great part by our relationships with others in the local fellowship (1 John 3:23; 4:7, 20). Specifically, how we *love one another*—commanded or implied seventeen times—is illuminated by over thirty commands to accept, edify, and submit to one another (as well as prohibitions regarding what not to do). As individual believers are being recreated in Christ's image, wrote Tertullian, so the church is being created in the Trinitarian image as "the body of the Three."[4]

Though programs cannot manufacture *koinonia*, alternative means to encourage fellowship can be fruitful. Methodist missionary E. Stanley Jones opened his spiritual retreats *(ashrams)* with "The Morning of the Heart," in which each person would share her or his needs. Often for

---

4. See John 17:20–23; Tertullian, *De baptismo*, 6.1.

four or five hours, believers would open their hearts to one another, sharing their pain and struggles as well as their joys. One first-time member reacted, "Good gracious, have we all the disrupted people in the country here?" Jones responded that, to the contrary, these hours of transparency revealed a cross-section of honest Christian life that is ordinarily suppressed by our craving to be respectable in our local church.

Deeper connectedness with other believers in the Lord cannot be orchestrated; it is dependent on the Holy Spirit himself. At the same time, we should pray and think through with others in our local church how to create conditions for genuine *koinonia*. At a singles' retreat given to study the meaning of "serving one another," a devotional study invited the washing of each other's feet. No ritual was intended, but only an approximation of Jesus' example (John 13:4–15), and no special arrangements were made this bright Sunday morning near the beach. A circle of maybe thirty stood in the grass surrounding a hose, a sponge, and a bar of soap, as a humble young man initiated the activity that would conclude our weekend. Few will forget what the Lord did that day. One twenty-something young woman took the hand of another and led her to the middle of the circle. As she washed the other's feet, she broke down in tears and asked forgiveness for her jealousy and gossip. The two embraced as the other woman confessed her belittling attitude and meanness. The second then washed the first woman's feet. A pastor took his six-year-old son to the center and cleaned his feet, vowing to be a better father in the Lord.

As the foot-washing continued, a rather tough young man stood outside the circle, seemingly disinterested in the whole affair. Toward the end of the time, one of the guys took his arm, brought him to the center, and washed his feet with verbal affirmation of Christian love. The young man was emotionally overwhelmed and wept openly. He had never before been so accepted and loved. Over the past several years, this precious brother has ministered as a missionary in various regions of the world, from the Peruvian Amazon to the cities of Siberia.

Through prayer and creative planning, the local church can and must pioneer forms to encourage serious *koinonia*. Love for one another is the most disarming and convincing of all apologetics before a skeptical world (John 13:35). Fellowship reveals the love of God through loving one another. It anticipates the heavenly community in which all Christians will share. House groups, "cell groups," and retreats are potent antidotes to the disconnected urban realities of the postmodern world. In particular, small groups can provide ongoing inductive Bible study, genuine sharing, and prayer that continue throughout the week. Settings like these foster *koinonia* by encouraging relational bonds that otherwise would not form in our busy lives.

Yet more can be done. Whether a work project to help repair the house of a needy widow or an all-night prayer vigil to intercede for unbelieving friends, whether a support group for parents struggling with their adolescent children or a pact of commitment to take the gospel to a resistant part of the world, the possibilities to experience biblical *koinonia* are endless. By whatever means we pursue fellowship, we must get beyond the superficial. We must ask the Lord for fresh ways to make our relationships more substantial and Christlike. The bottom line is that, in light of Scripture, if a local congregation is not experiencing deep fellowship among its members, then it fails to function as the Lord of the church has intended. In that sense, it disqualifies itself spiritually as a New Testament church.

Evangelism/Mission

In his last words prior to his ascension into heaven, Jesus commissioned his followers to spread the gospel throughout the world (Acts 1:8; Matt. 28:19–20). At Pentecost, Peter publicly preached the gospel in Jerusalem, and three thousand people were baptized. Luke records that these first Christians enjoyed "the favor of all the people. And the Lord added to their number daily those who were being saved" (Acts 2:47). Acts records the failures as well as the unction of the early church in spreading the good news through courageous testimony, open preaching, apologetic debate, missionary travels, and martyrdom. The New Testament also reveals less explicit forms of evangelism: doing good to others (Titus 3:1–2, 8, 14); sharing of possessions (Heb. 13:16); exemplary conduct in the midst of unbelievers (1 Peter 2:12); and readiness of response to those who ask about the reason for one's hope (1 Peter 3:15). Especially powerful is the infectious attraction of the communal life of the early church, even with its problems. The local church's very way of being—its vitality of worship, growth in understanding, and fellowship—can itself be evangelistic. The collective testimony of believers is designed to attract non-Christians who are seeking spiritual authenticity. Amid the plurality of cultures through world history, diverse methods of evangelism have been used to disseminate the gospel, make disciples, and start new local churches. After the New Testament era, followers of Christ continued their testimony through public preaching, sacrificially giving possessions to the poor, and establishing orphanages and hospices. In the sixth and seventh centuries, dozens of Irish monks traveled two-by-two from the tiny island of Iona, with little more than the clothes on their backs, proclaiming the gospel through Scotland and northern England. Likewise, Nestorian missionaries pressed eastward in the seventh and eighth centuries, boldly proclaiming Christianity into the heart of China, winning converts even in the family of the emperor in Ch'ang-an, which at the time was probably the largest city in the world. Social historian Philip Jenkins argues that the West has seriously underestimated the strength and expansion of medieval Christianity in Asia and Africa. By the year 1200, Africa likely had five million Christians and Asia more than forty million, nearly the same number as in Europe and Russia combined.[5] Over the past two thousand years, evangelism and mission have been characterized by various periods of creativity and zeal.

In the twentieth century, various North American evangelists—notably Billy Graham—appropriated radio, television, cinema, and especially crusade evangelism to spread the gospel of Christ. Bible, tract, and book distribution has likewise strengthened the church's witness, including worldwide use of *The Four Spiritual Laws* booklet in one-on-one evangelism. Others prefer door-to-door visitation, telephone ministries, Internet dialogue, or music concerts ranging from gospel to pop to hard rock. Increasingly among adults in Europe and North America, public evangelism appears less effective in communicating the gospel than relational efforts to establish friendship and trust. Younger generations also yearn for meaningful spiritual engagement on personal and relational

---

5. Philip Jenkins, *The Next Christendom: The Coming of Global Christianity* (Oxford: Oxford University Press, 2002), 23–24.

levels. Today evangelism is often understood in the broad terms of *mission*, defined as "seeking to restore in Christ all that has been destroyed by sin." Hence, thousands of social ministries complement direct evangelism in the proclamation of the gospel.

In the midst of these efforts, the greatest sociological movement of the twentieth century was not the rise and fall of communism but the massive pendulum sweep of Christianity into the Third World. In 1900, colonial Africa had only 8.7 million Christians, about nine percent of the people—and mostly Coptic or Ethiopian Orthodox. At the same time, Muslims were 34.5 million strong. By 1985, more than 16,500 Christian conversions a day were occurring in Africa, even as 4,300 were abandoning Christendom in Europe and North America.[6] According to the most reliable statistic available at this writing, Africa today boasts 360 million people considered "Christian," Asia has 327 million, and Latin America has another 498 million.[7] Never in the history of the world has the gospel of Jesus Christ been proclaimed to such a proportionately massive percentage of people.

Evangelism and mission are the great commission of all the body of Christ, not only of those on the frontiers of Christian mission. The church is called to both creativity and courage. Whatever the forms of legitimate persuasion, all serve as means to present Jesus Christ as the Savior of mankind. Evangelistic forms must reach, by the power of the Spirit, subcultures as diverse as humanity itself, from tribal animists in Surinam to Muslim youth in Indonesia; from factory workers in Beijing to AIDS victims in Vancouver, B.C., to Jewish senior citizens in Dade County, Florida.

Obedience to the gospel brings the Cross into the lives of Christians. As we enter the religious tensions of the twenty-first century, heaven itself is witness to the hundreds of thousands, quite possibly millions, of

---

6. Lamin Sanneh, *Whose Religion Is Christianity? The Gospel Beyond the West* (Grand Rapids: Eerdmans, 2003), 14–15.

7. David B. Barrett and Todd M. Johnson, "Annual Statistical Table on Global Mission: 2004," *International Bulletin of Missionary Research*, 28, no. 1 (January 2004), 25. This is an update of D. Barrett, George T. Kurian, and Todd M. Johnson, eds., *World Christian Encyclopedia: A Comparative Survey of Churches and Religions from ad 30–ad 2000*, 2 vols. (2d. ed., Oxford: Oxford University Press, 2001).

believers in the past one hundred years who were faithful to the point of death under regimes hostile to Christian faith.[8] The Korean awakening to evangelical faith occurred in the 1920s and 1930s, predominantly in the north. After the communist invasion and eventual division from South Korea in 1948, tens of thousands of Christians appear to have been exterminated, a political agenda that seems to continue yet today. The writer of Hebrews reminds us that "a great cloud of witnesses" surrounds believers, all the more reason to "fix our eyes on Jesus, the author and perfecter of our faith, who for the joy set before him endured the cross" (Heb. 12:2). A church without evangelism is a church without the Cross. However diverse its means, however successful its results, evangelism is an essential activity of the New Testament church.

The local church is composed of *professing believers in Jesus Christ who have been baptized, practice the Lord's Supper, and organize to do God's will.* We have defined "God's will" by four basic functions of the church: worship, learning, fellowship, and evangelism/mission. These distill the multitude of activities of the local church, summarizing what members should be experiencing and doing, complemented by scriptural directives regarding baptism, the Lord's Supper, qualified leadership, and the discipline of wayward members.

The way in which our Lord works through the church, as distinguished from Old Testament Israel, is essentially decentralized. The local church does not exist to concentrate all the energy and service of the Christian community in its own activities. Rather, it exists to prepare individual believers to better shine forth as spiritual lights in their homes, neighborhoods, schools, workplaces, and communities. Rather than binding its most faithful members to itself, the local church equips and liberates its participants to better serve God not only in the church but also in the world.

---

8. Ibid., estimates over 160,000 Christian martyrs per year currently; the average numbers in 1970 were 377,000 per year; in 1900, less than 35,000.

Chapter 7

ROAD POSTS TOWARD A NEW TESTAMENT CHURCH

Where snow falls deep in some parts of North America, occasionally one observes highway markers or road posts that help operators of snowplows determine the course of the road. In the Plains States after a heavy snowfall, a highway can disappear altogether if not for markers (or at least telephone poles) to guide the way. In the Cascade Mountains of the Pacific Northwest, a simple road post might keep a snow-equipment operator from plunging to his death down a ravine. Road posts are set deeply into the ground and rise tall to withstand the vicissitudes of weather and time. They exist to help keep us on the road when it's hard to see where we are going.

The purpose of our study has been to define road posts from the New Testament that set us on course toward becoming the church that God desires. Our brief theological treatment has attempted to clarify these biblical markers that guide the way. We saw that the New Testament employs *ekklesia* in two primary ways: as *local church* and *universal church*. The *local church,* in its earthy, practical sense, is a group of professing believers in Christ who have been baptized, practice the Lord's Supper, and who organize to do God's will. Descriptions of the local churches in the first century reveal members and situations that are far from ideal. This kind of biblical realism invites us to recognize that we too are far from perfect, and that every congregation will have to cope with awkward or troublesome situations. But the road posts along the snowy highway are clearly in sight as we move toward what the New Testament sets forth for the local church.

If the local church may be defined pragmatically, the *universal church* generally cannot. The universal church is the spiritual entity that includes all those regenerate in Christ and indwelled by the Holy Spirit. Whether we prefer Paul's phrase "the body of Christ" or Peter's "royal priesthood," this ultimate and true church is the absolute that gives purpose and place to local congregations. That is, local churches should be measured in light of the overarching reality of the universal church.

If what we have seen reflects the doctrinal framework of the *ekklesia* in the New Testament, then what might it mean for specific congregations? The following suggestions can help churches better evaluate their forms and activities before the mirror of Scripture.

The Essence of the Local Church

The purpose of the local church is to do God's will. We can clarify and often simplify the reasons for assembling as a group of believers by asking, Why do we exist as a local church? God's will is not centered in buildings, special Sabbaths of worship, high-octane services, or professional leadership. Rather, four functions observable in the newborn church of Acts 2 proliferate throughout the rest of the New Testament. These activities make tangible the outworking of God's regenerative power in his people: worship, learning, fellowship, and evangelism/mission. Some congregations may prefer to divide New Testament functions differently. However one might categorize them, it is essential to define the functions of the local church from the Bible itself, rather than from habit, tradition, or what other people expect a church to look like. Describing afresh what our own local church is all about, revisiting old purpose statements, and reconceiving how we think of the *ekklesia* can breathe life into a tired congregation. Thus, the first step toward rethinking the church from a New Testament perspective involves a fresh articulation of the *why* of one's church. What is the reason for and the essence of our local congregation's existence? For some, such a step will already seem revolutionary.

Forms Without Function

Two more questions are fundamental: *Are the forms of our church functioning? Do they fulfill the purposes of the church?* If a local church is not developing as its own priorities the central functions of the New Testament church, it stands outside God's will and purpose. A local church is like a human body. Without essential biblical activities, a church is either asleep or paralyzed. Indeed, without *any* vital signs at all, it is clinically dead.

The New Testament does not deny that a passive congregation—such as the lukewarm assembly at Laodicea (Rev. 3:14–22)—can be a "church" in a formal or external sense. But just as an individual believer who regresses into carnality becomes in a practical sense a Christian in name only, a congregation that does not evince the presence of the living God becomes a church in form only. Just as a lifeless corpse is no longer a human being, an ecclesiastical form without spiritual life is no longer a viable New Testament church. Without the indispensable spiritual functions of worship, learning, fellowship, and evangelism/mission, a church loses its vital signs, its soul, its experiential identity, its *raison d'etre*.

Dysfunctional Churches

Churches, and even entire denominations, often overemphasize certain New Testament functions at the expense of others. Like an out-of-tune four-cylinder engine being coaxed along, coughing and backfiring, such churches sputter along with only three, two, or even one cylinder functioning well. Traditional High Churches are known for their worshipful liturgy, yet they can be devoid of evangelism, deeper fellowship, or even life-changing learning. Some churches emphasize only evangelism but engage in little worship, biblical learning, or intimate *koinonia*. Others prioritize fellowship among members but are anemic in areas of local outreach, equipping, or rendering glory to Almighty God. Certain of these groups separate themselves so entirely from "the world" that they become cultural oddities in society, without mission in the world and no longer offering any feasible option for the unbelieving seeker. Still other local churches emphasize theology and Bible knowledge, but they lack heartfelt worship, true fellowship, or courage in evangelism. Surely there will always be diversity among God's people. Church names dot the maps of most major cities of the world, each with its own history and tradition—Holy Trinity Episcopal Cathedral, North Village Assembly of God, St. Matthew's Methodist Church, Smithville Community Fellowship, Our Savior's Presbyterian Church, and Calvary Outreach Center. Though each church will reflect its own personality and healthy identity, it cannot be content to ignore the primary functions for which each local church exists. Rather, every congregation must seek an active biblical balance reflective of the dynamic functions of the New Testament church.

How Do We Begin?

As a leadership team, Bible study group, or entire local assembly, a group of believers can start by conducting an honest self-evaluation of its church's activities in light of the biblical functions of the *ekklesia*. What is the congregation doing that parallels the activities of the early church? What appears to be peripheral? Where are there noticeable gaps between normative New Testament functions and our own? Obviously, methodologies and culturally specific forms of activities will vary, and may vary quite a lot. The point is, how do these line up with the primary functions in Scripture? Through a self-evaluation process, a local congregation's activities can be compared and contrasted with those of the early church, identifying strengths and clarifying weaknesses to be brought before the Lord. Recentering our local churches within New Testament principles does not mean we jettison every form and practice of our denomination, tradition, or pattern. Our history is part of who we are. Our creative responses to New Testament imperatives will build on our strengths as a local church. Rejuvenation does not mean we depart from the character of who we are as a specific group of believers. Oriented by Scripture and led by the Holy Spirit, we can then begin to take specific steps within our local congregation toward balancing and developing our activities in light of the main themes visible in the early churches. Yet this involves additional considerations.

Function Before Form

In contrast to the carefully prescribed external forms given to ancient Israel, New Testament ecclesiastical forms exist to accomplish the primary roles prescribed for the church. This is not to say that certain unifying forms of baptism, the Lord's Supper, and qualified leadership do not remain in place. But beyond these minimal prescriptions that unite all true Christian assemblies, the church's organization, structure, liturgies, and music are to be deliberately flexible in order to accomplish the transgenerational and transcultural functions of the church.

God designed the local church like an exoskeletal animal. A crab's outer shell must be regularly discarded so that the life within can grow, adapt, and recreate larger new forms. Those forms may be our liturgies, music, regular programs, organization, financial commitments, and even our buildings. Some leaders fight to maintain those shells at all costs, even as the spiritual vitality of the members wanes and dies. Not a few cathedrals—now elaborate shells of once dynamic churches—are scattered across Christendom today. The exoskeleton was preserved while, in too many congregations, the spiritual life within perished. True spiritual life within a congregation cannot remain still. The life of the God of the Bible repeatedly breaks forth in surprising if not innovative forms. Those who think otherwise need only look at history.

If a church lacks experiential worship of God, grasping Christian truths, substantial fellowship, or witness with new people coming to Christ, then something is wrong. The problems, obviously, are not always in terms of forms and activities. The empowering grace of God will not be present where pride, laziness, immorality, or other unrighteousness displeases his Holy Spirit. Sin must surely be dealt with in the local congregation.

Other times, however, the very way we "do church"—the accumulation of forms by which we express our faith—is itself the barrier that prohibits our reaching New Testament goals. A church should be free to change its external forms to better accomplish God's priorities. Adaptation is necessary both to maximize the functions of the local church and to better communicate the truths of the gospel in diverse contexts. An African should not be obliged to wear a suit and tie to the village church. A Latin American congregation should not assume that good evangelical churches worship at 10 AM on Sunday mornings. While we must guard biblical teaching and sound doctrine, and while we retain the best of our ecclesiastical traditions, we *must*—we are *obligated*—to reevaluate the forms of the local church for each culture and generation. If we do not, the way we embody the message of Christ becomes irrelevant and no longer incarnational. That God became man and lived among us, being "made like his brothers in every way" (Heb. 2:17), and that Paul became "all things to all men so that [he] by all possible means . . . might save some" (1 Cor. 9:22), suggest that the forms of our churches should "fit" among the people to whom the local church is called to be salt and light. Churches, in a sense, have no right to ask new converts to join a subculture wholly foreign to everything they have ever known. The love of Christ constrains us to develop forms in the local church that maximize the biblical functions of the church in ways that harmonize as much as possible with the culture God has called us to reach.

In light of the various patterns and activities of our churches, we would do well to stop and ask ourselves some hard questions. How many hours are spent in committee meetings to preserve the ecclesiastical bureaucracy? What percentage of our human and financial resources are spent constructing and maintaining the church's building, parking lot, and real estate? What about the choir, youth bands, singing groups, or church orchestras? Are thousands of hours of collective effort and tens of thousands of dollars well spent in these areas in light of New Testament priorities? What about the sports programs? Youth outings? Christian conventions? Group mission trips? Each church should judge itself before Scripture. Hundreds of activities fill the typical church's monthly calendar. Congregations can invest quite a lot of energy toward activities that contribute little or nothing to the church's role as the body of Christ in the world. A generation ago, Francis Schaeffer decried the wasted "churchiness" of much of evangelicalism. His words ring true yet today:

> We must have the courage to change all kinds of things in our services. Stay within the limits of the form of the New Testament, but count everything else free under the leadership of the Holy Spirit. Begin to talk to your boards, begin to talk to your session, have prayer meetings about what you can change

in your service to make our churches living things in the generation which we are facing.

Furthermore, you can quit having so many meaningless meetings in your church. You can eliminate those that meant something yesterday but not today, and then officers and people can spend more time opening their homes to other people. Not just so everyone can sit with their feet up and watch the little black box for three more hours. But so that you can talk to your children about the things they need to know in such a day as ours, have some family life, read to your children. Then you can open your home to a wider community. There are dozens of meetings in almost every church that could just as well be scrapped—meetings that have nothing to do with the norms of Scripture and therefore are not sacred as such.

It isn't too hard to begin. Of course, as soon as you start, it will be difficult because often you will have to buck the evangelical establishment. . . .

We need to teach a Christianity of content and purity of doctrine. And we must be free to change those things in our church polity and practice which need changing.[1]

Perhaps the worst consequence of an overbooked church calendar is that it communicates to our members and to the unbelieving world that *this* is how we serve God; that involvement in church programs is the measure of Christian spirituality; that motion equals ministry; that being religious is the same as being Christian. Rather than equipping believers to *be* the body of Christ in the midst of the world, sometimes the local church becomes the greatest hindrance of all.

Creativity and Denominationalism

This book was born outside the United States in several settings of what might approach a kind of denominational tribalism. Sometimes

---

1. Francis A. Schaeffer, *The Church at the End of the Twentieth Century* (Downers Grove, Ill.: InterVarsity, 1970), 110–11.

powerful chieftains, suspicious of other denominations, dictate to those under their authority every detail of a church's form and activity. Although not normally the case, wherever in the world, denominational leaders and even pastors can overstep their bounds.

Are denominational organizations helpful? In North America over the last decade, at least one major consultation of religious leaders has concluded that although denominational structures were advantageous in the past, they are increasingly unnecessary and irrelevant. Others would argue that such a judgment is premature. Although denominational organizations are perhaps not essential to local congregations, they still play a positive role in the coordination and supervision of local churches. One compelling reason for denominational affiliation is purity of doctrine. Independent churches are more susceptible to invention or changes of what was once sound theology, typically around the persuasions of an energetic leader. Some of the largest churches in the world today proclaim teachings that would be seen as heresy by almost all of historic Christianity. My own experience suggests that denominational leadership is especially helpful in the developing countries, where resources are not readily available and doctrine is often undefined.

Nevertheless, the opposite can also be true: denominational leadership can betray biblical commitments. When an organization's teachings become unfaithful to historic Christian faith and its founding creeds, they become like wooden pilings along the seashore that, though they appear solid from above, have rotted out below the waterline. When divinity schools and organizational leadership no longer embrace classical Christian doctrine, whole families of churches are swept to sea with the rise and fall of cultural tides. But if a denomination is firm theologically under the authority of Scripture, then its churches have moorings and structure for truth and a future.

Denominational affiliations also provide a structure of accountability and a moral safety net. Witness the cycle of television evangelists over the past thirty years, one after another who peaked and then collapsed under the weight of an unbridled desire for greatness, webs of deception, and secret sin. One is reminded of spacious church edifices and whole Christian campuses that sit empty, having been built on the dreams of visionaries with minimal accountability. Denominational structures can nurture righteous standards in their leaders and churches, and they can strengthen congregations through times of moral failure without an utter loss of all that is involved.

To be sure, denominational traditions have made valuable contributions in areas of doctrine and practice. Nevertheless, as argued above, the New Testament is largely nonprescriptive regarding post-apostolic leadership beyond the local church. God's Word allows for organizational freedom within the parameters of a few New Testament absolutes. Denominational institutions, programs, models, liturgies, styles, hymnbooks, and literature will eventually be forgotten. History shows that so much of what has consumed enormous ecclesial effort and often large sums of money will sooner or later become obsolete. Though attitudes are changing, denominational leaders have too easily assumed that what they accomplish will continue for generations to come. Today, such an assumption can rarely be justified. Defending traditional forms and structures, some find themselves frustrated when younger leaders are not convinced that such externals are any longer meaningful.

Other than the covenantal signs of baptism and the Lord's Supper, God did not design rites for the local church to perpetuate. Indeed, if the church is to express sound doctrine in new ways and experience the powerful functions that are central to its existence, it cannot be tied down static forms. When a tradition becomes inefficient in accomplishing the purposes of God, it is necessary to change it or discard it altogether. Critical thinking is required in evaluating denominational goals, priorities, and politics in light of Scripture. Rather than repress innovation of new forms, denominations would do well to nourish biblical experimentation to discover more efficient and more relevant ways to fulfill God's purpose for the local church. Indeed, championing creative ecclesiology provides denominations themselves with future options for what their churches can become. Otherwise, the pattern of history is that denominations lose the essence of the church by trying to preserve their forms and traditions. When patterns and structures of the church are set in stone, when the shell becomes the absolute, the creative life within breathes its last.

The Churches and the Church

The universal church, the body of Christ, exists as the overarching reality by which we determine the place and value of the local church. Each local congregation participates in the absolute church to the extent that its members are truly regenerate and continue in active relationship with the Head of the church. Regardless of their differences, every biblically authentic local church belongs to a global family of congregations that serve as the body of Christ in the world.

Two implications are clear. First, at the individual level, if I cannot experience interdenominational *koinonia* with other genuine Christians, then sin is present either in my life or the other person's. This is not to say that discipline or breaking fellowship is unwarranted when a professing believer has decidedly turned from "the Way" to the world. But it does mean that as a believer I can have, and should have, fellowship with others who have placed their trust in Jesus Christ, regardless of our denominational differences. Under Christ's headship over his church, we are brought into oneness of spirit in the midst of our diversities.

Second, at the ecclesiastical level we must remember that no local congregation perfectly represents the body of Christ. On a ten-point scale, one church may score a nine, another a seven, and still another perhaps a three. But no local church gets a perfect ten. Instead of comparing ourselves with neighboring churches of regenerate believers, criticizing them or prohibiting our members from having fellowship with them, we have every theological reason for helping one another—just as within a single congregation a stronger brother should help a weaker one. This does not imply ecumenical unification that compromises doctrine in order to merge with others who also call themselves Christian. We can maintain our distinctions and convictions as God has directed. I am not suggesting, of course, that our generosity of fellowship enfold cults or obscure the line between Christian orthodoxy and false teaching. Those who deny the Triune God, the two natures of Jesus Christ, the substitutionary death of Christ, and the final authority of Scripture are outside historical and biblical Christian faith.

But when we understand the true church as the body of Christ uniting all born-again believers, our attitude changes, especially toward other evangelical or "Great Commission" churches. They are not the enemy. Rather, other churches of regenerate believers are groups with experiences and traditions different from ours, yet who are seeking, as we are, to accomplish God's will in the world. Therefore, church leaders can take the initiative to help other churches. And we can receive help from other churches without fear. Something far greater than our differences is at stake. Every person who is born again belongs to the body of Christ. To reject fellowship with a brother or sister—one who is reasonably faithful to basic doctrine and walking in the light of Christ—is to reject fellowship with Christ himself.

A Decentralized Vision for the Local Church

Contrary to the working of the kingdom of God in the Old Testament, which was oriented to one people group, one geographic center, one day of the week, and one priestly caste, the new entity of the church as the body of Christ inverts a centralized vision to one encouraging an outflowing movement to all peoples and places. As a finite expression of the body of Christ, the local church is designed to reflect this decentralizing perspective by penetrating the community in which it lives. As a local church moves out from itself, evangelism and missions are immediately implied.

Decentralization of the energy and form of the church, however, suggests much more than attention to evangelism and missions. How many of our members work five or six days a week, to then attend church on Sunday morning, spend the afternoon in visitation or choir practice, and finally attend the evening service or youth activities, only to return to work on Monday simply worn out? A decentralized vision emphasizes that the church is not the center of everything for the Christian life. It does not absorb all the energy of its members in its own activities. Rather, the local church should teach its members to feed daily on the Word of God and to enter directly into the Lord's presence, then throughout the week to assume their place as priests of the Most High God. Members should be encouraged to nurture meaningful times with their spouses, children, parents, and relatives. Churches should help members to befriend their neighbors and to communicate the gospel to friends, or to open their homes to others, providing genuine, friendly, convincing testimony. A decentralizing perspective means that church leaders draw in members to prepare them for ministry, and then send them out again as Christ's presence in people's lives outside the church. Rather than being a convent that removes Christians from the world, the church should become a support network and spiritual family for every member's ministry. The local church exists as a *means* to perfect believers and their ministries in service to Christ, not as an *end* in itself.

New Forms and Unchanging Doctrine

While emphasizing the freedom of form for the local church, I would insist again that *ekklesial* liberty derives from the Word of God itself, our authority and compass for the truly important. Local church forms will vary, but the constant *message* of the local church is the teaching of Scripture. Though the application of biblical truth will vary across generations and cultures, Christian doctrine is the bedrock of the Christian faith. We resist any inference that the Bible is no longer adequate or, specifically, that its normative teaching is no longer appropriate for the church. To the contrary, the fact that the Bible is our supreme authority is what frees us to return to Scripture and rediscover truths about the church that have been obscured by tradition and custom. One reason why many believers fear change and defend local church traditions is because they suspect that change leads away from truth rather than toward it. Despite good intentions, pastors and Christian leaders sometimes resist change not because they know the Bible but because they do *not* know the New Testament teaching regarding the *ekklesia*. As the church becomes more biblical, it also can become more resplendent in what God has called it to do.

THE END OR A NEW BEGINNING?

In naturalist Jean-Henri Fabre's experiment, the processionary caterpillars continued their same path around the mouth of the vase until they became exhausted and died. In our local churches, is it possible we are working in vain rather than fulfilling God's purpose for our congregations? Our activities and even our successes can deceive us.

What would the external forms of a church be without real estate? Without a "worship center"? Without Sunday set apart? Without preoccupation with programs and performances? Without professional clergy? Perhaps such a church would not be ideal. But it would in no sense less qualify as a New Testament church. Indeed, it would look quite a lot like suppressed and persecuted churches throughout the last century in China, North Korea, Vietnam, Indonesia, Pakistan, Russia, Romania, Iran, Saudi Arabia, Mozambique, Morocco, Cuba, and numerous other places where the church has suffered. Today, as well, underground Christian congregations in various parts of the world may be very much spiritually alive as they experience the same dynamic functions of worship, learning, fellowship, and evangelism found in the earliest church, yet in ways very different from our own.

No one can foretell what the twenty-first century will bring to Western Christianity. Our affluence and freedom may continue to give us enormous opportunities to employ our resources well for the kingdom of God.

Or perhaps not. Our challenge is not so much to prognosticate the future but to faithfully serve our Lord today. Whatever our role in a local church—as church-planter, pastor, lay-leader, or interested participant—let us do what we can to align our "doing church" with the true *ekklesia* of God. Our study has outlined a structural rather than a complete ecclesiology. We have examined the New Testament blueprints for constructing, or reconstructing, a church from the ground up. Many of the ideas are not new. But they are intended to contribute to the emergence of churches in the twenty-first century that have renewed perspective on their reason for existence and on the creative latitude that each church has regarding forms and modes of expression as granted by the risen Christ.

FOUR FUNCTIONS OR MORE?

In presenting these materials, I am occasionally asked why I include only four categories of functions: worship, learning, fellowship, and evangelism/mission. The four functions are meant to be inclusive, not exclusive. Some would add miracles, social action, or prayer to the list. Organization also is needed in the local church, as discussed, but administration is probably best seen as a necessary social function rather than a dynamic corporate experience. A few words about the other possibilities may help.

Miracles

Based on Acts 2 and other texts regarding the earliest church, some have included signs and wonders as a fifth activity of the church. Certainly such an argument takes seriously the miraculous power of the Holy Spirit among the first believers. Moreover, it directly challenges Christians today to exercise faith in prayer and evangelism for tangible divine intervention in the spiritual warfare of our time. However, rather than being a continual experience of all believers in all times and locations, miracles in the New Testament especially mark the ministry of the apostles (Heb. 2:3–4). Indeed, signs and wonders appear less predominant in the second half of Acts and in the later books of the New Testament—although exorcism of demons seems to have continued into the fourth century. This is not to deny the miraculous in the church throughout history and today, but simply to suggest that miracles are given by God to encourage the church and not as a weekly function in which all churches engage at all times.

Social Action

Others include social action as a normative function of the church. Interestingly, however, although every believer should be eager to do good works, the social action of the New Testament church seems especially (not exclusively) related to those within the body of Christ. Early believers were encouraged to help needy orphans, widows, and the poor, particularly those who believed (James 1:27; Matt. 25:31–46). Churches are urged to aid congregations in other regions of the world that are suffering, as seen in the collections for the church in Palestine (1 Cor. 16:1–3; 2 Cor. 8:1–20). In a similar manner, local churches are invited to support missionaries like Paul, Apollos, and Titus (Phil. 2:25; 4:14–18). Christians are warned not to love in word only; rather, true love for a needy believer evokes activity regarding the whole person (1 John 3:17–18). It is true that as a persecuted minority, the New Testament church may not have had resources to do much more than survive. For whatever reason, the epistles never directly call local churches to collective social outreach to unbelievers. Though Paul gathered apparently generous funds to help the Jerusalem saints, no record in the New Testament describes church offerings for the non-Christian world. Rather, the model appears to have been *individual* goodwill, as reflected in Jesus' parable of the Good Samaritan. Whereas certain principles might encourage a church to develop social programs, the New Testament reflects, again, a decentralized pattern of outreach rather than establishing the local church itself as an institutional center for social programs. Whatever one's opinion of the place of social programs in the life of the church, helping the needy fits into both categories of *koinonia* and evangelism/mission. Social outreach is the obligation of every believer, but it may be best identified as a corollary of fellowship (caring for one another) and/or evangelism (communicating the good news of Christ in the world). This is not to say that doing good to others has no value in itself (for that is what God does).

The point is that collective social action is not a primary function of the local church in the New Testament in the sense of worship, teaching/learning, fellowship, and evangelism.

Prayer

Others have suggested that prayer should be a vital function of the local church as immediately evident in Acts 2. In one sense, who can deny the centrality of the church gathering to pray? From my perspective, prayer spreads across all the categories. True worship is always prayerful if not expressed in prayer itself. True fellowship directly involves intercession for one another, both in assembly and in private. If the Holy Spirit is our teacher, how can teaching and comprehending spiritual truths occur without invoking God's presence? Godly teaching is directed horizontally to others yet also upwardly in prayer. Evangelism depends entirely on prayer for prepared hearts, boldness in proclamation, protection of the messengers, and fruitfulness of harvest. We must pray, for that is our walking relationship with the Lord. Therefore, just as speech itself, prayer pertains to *all* the basic functions of the church.

Conclusion

Thus, I conclude that the dozens of activities of the New Testament church fall into the four primary functions of worship, learning, fellowship, and evangelism/mission. Without diminishing the Lord's power to do miracles, the believer's bidding to engage in good works, or the value and necessity of prayer, the four big categories include all the positive activities that incarnate the will of God for the church.

SUGGESTED READING

Berry, Carmen Renee. *The Unauthorized Guide to Choosing a Church.* Grand Rapids: Baker (Brazos), 2003.

Driver, John. *Images of the Church in Mission.* Scottsdale, Pa.: Herald Press, 1997.

Evans, Tony. *God's Glorious Church: The Mystery and Mission of the Body of Christ.* Chicago: Moody, 2003.

Frost, Michael. *Shaping of Things to Come: Innovation and Mission for the 21st Century Church.* Peabody, Mass.: Hendrickson, 2003.

Getz, Gene A. *Elders and Leaders: God's Plan for Leading the Church: A Biblical, Historical and Cultural Perspective.* Chicago: Moody, 2003.

———*Sharpening the Focus of the Church.* Wheaton, Ill.: Victor Books, 1984.

Jenkins, Philip. *The Next Christendom: The Coming of Global Christianity.* Oxford: Oxford University Press, 2002.

MacArthur, John, Jr. *The Church: The Body of Christ: Study Notes.* Edited by David Sper. Sun Valley, Calif.: Word of Grace Communications, 1981.

Malphurs, Aubrey. *Doing Church: A Biblical Guide for Leading Ministries Through Change.* Grand Rapids: Kregel, 1999.

Petersen, Jim. *Church Without Walls: Moving Beyond Traditional Boundaries.* Colorado Springs: NavPress, 1992.

Ryken, Philip Graham. *City on a Hill: Reclaiming the Biblical Pattern of the Church for the 21st Century.* Chicago: Moody, 2003.

Saucy, Robert L. *The Church in God's Program.* Chicago: Moody, 1972.

Schaeffer, Francis A. *The Church at the End of the Twentieth Century.* Downers Grove, Ill.: InterVarsity, 1970.

Snyder, Howard A. *Radical Renewal: The Problem of Wine Skins.* Rev. ed. Houston: Touch Publications, 1996.

Stedman, Ray C. *Body Life.* Glendale, Calif.: Regal, 1972.

Thompson, Paul, et al. *What Does It Mean to Be a World Christian?* Coral Gables, Fla., and Warrington, Pa.: Worldteam, 1978.

Tillapaugh, Frank R. *The Church Unleashed: Getting God's People Out Where the Needs Are.* Ventura, Calif.: Regal, 1982.

Van Gelder, Craig. *The Essence of the Church: A Community Created by the Spirit.* Grand Rapids: Baker, 2000.

Warren, Rick. *The Purpose-Driven Church: Growth Without Compromising Your Message and Mission.* Grand Rapids: Zondervan, 1995.

SCRIPTURE INDEX

Genesis
2:2–3 . . . . 46, 57
12:1–3 42
15:4–22 42
17:3–8, 15–19 42
22:15–18 42

Exodus
16:22–30 47
16:23–30 43
20:8–11 . . . . 31, 47
20:8–12 43
20:22 47
31:12–17 42

Numbers
14:3–4 25

Deuteronomy
7:3 42

Judges
20:2 33

1 Samuel
13:8–14 43

2 Samuel
14:13 33

1 Kings
11:1–2 42

1 Chronicles
16:28–29 42

Nehemiah
9:13–14 47
9:14 43

Job
1:6 34
2:1 34

Psalms
22:22 24
89:5, 7 34
96:7–8 42

Jeremiah
31:33 37

Ezekiel
20:12–21 43

Zechariah
14:5 34

Matthew
3:11 37
11:11 32
11:13 32
13:24–30 64
16:18 . . . . 25, 27, 36
18:17 25
22:29–32, 43–45 66
24:35 66
25:31 34
25:31–46 102
26:26–29 68
28:19 . . . . 45, 47, 67
28:19–20 . . . . 78, 82

Luke
7:28 33
22:14–20 68

John
10:35 66
13:4–15 81
13:35 81
14:16–17 36
16:13 66
16:14 70
17:20–23 80

Acts
1:5 36
1:8 . . . . 45, 82
2 . . . . 36, 73, 88,
    101, 103
2:1–4 36
2:42 . . . . . 65, 74, 76, 79
2:42–47 73
2:43 74
2:44 79
2:46 . . . . . 53, 68, 74, 79
2:47 . . . . 74, 82
4:23–31 74
6:1–7 53
6:7 78
7:38 24
8:1 26
8:38–39 67
9:31 26
11:15–16 37
11:22, 26 26
13:2–3 74
15:1–31 46
15:28 46
18:24–28 77
19:32, 41 25
20:7 . . . . 47, 68
20:11 68
20:17, 28 49

Romans
11:33 35
12:2 77
12:13 34
14:5 48
16:1 26

1 Corinthians
3:9 46
3:10–15 71
3:16–17 46
4:14–15 71
6:19 46
9:22 92
10:16 68
11:3, 10 49
11:16 26
11:18 25
11:20 68
11:22 26
11:23–26 . . . . . . 47, 68
11:23–33 74
11:24 68
12:7–11 71
12:12–27 . . . . . . 27, 38
12:13 37
14:4 25
14:19 25
14:28 . . . . 25, 71
14:30 71
14:32 71
14:34 25
14:40 71
15:24–28 70
16:1 34
16:1–3 102
16:2 47
16:19 26

2 Corinthians
1:1 26
8:1–20 102

9:12 34
12:14 71

Galatians
1:2 26
3:26–4:7 44
4:8–11 48
4:19 71

Ephesians
1:9–10 32
1:13–14 37
1:22–23 . . . . 27, 38
2:19 33–34
2:20 36
3:3–5 32
3:6 32
3:8 34
3:9–10 32
4:11–13 77
4:11–16 49
4:12 34
4:15–16 . . . . 27, 38
5:18–20 74
6:18 74

Philippians
2:24 102
3:5–6 29
4:14–18 102

Colossians
1:18, 24 . . . . 27, 38
2:5 71
2:16–17 48
3:16 74

1 Thessalonians
1:1 26
2:11 71

1 Timothy
2:11–14 49
2:24 26
3:1–10 54
3:8–12 49
4:1–11 65
4:16 . . . . 65, 77

Titus
1:5–9 54
1:9 65
2:1 . . . . 65, 77
3:1–2, 8, 14 82

Hebrews
1:1–3 66
2:3–4 101
2:12 24
2:17 92
4:9 33
8:8–12 37
10:24–25 48
12:2 85
12:22–23 34
12:28 27
13:16 82
13:24 34

James
1:27 102
5:14 26

1 Peter
2:5 . . . . 27, 49
2:5–7 46
2:6 36
2:9 . . . . 27, 44
2:10 33
2:12 82
3:15 82
5:1–4 49

2 Peter
2:1–22 65
3:15–16 66

1 John
1:3, 6–7 79
3:17–18 102
3:23 80
4:7, 20 80

3 John 25

Jude
3 . . . . 65, 77

Revelation
1–3 25
1:5–6 27
1:6 49
1:10 47
2–3 . . . . 26, 71
3:14–22 89
5:11–13 34
22:16–19 66
22:21 34